Bougainvillea

and
Other Stories

Bougainvillea
and
Other Stories

Bitan Chakraborty

Translated by
Pranab Ghosh

First published in India in May, 2016 by
Shambhabi – The Third Eye Imprint,
A-10/1, Amarabati, Sodepur,
Calcutta 700110

Printed and bound at S.P. Communication,
Garpar Road, Calcutta.

Cover photograph courtesy: Mary Torregrossa

Cover illustration & design: *Chitrangi*

ISBN-13: 97893-85783-99-9

Price: INR Two hundred only [Rs.200/- only]

Downtrodden people, middle class and lower middle class Bengali families and their lives have been my inspiration. We essentially ignore the basics of Indian constitution that has been primarily formed to protect and uplift the interests of the underprivileged.

—*Bitan Chakraborty*

Chakraborty: The Magic of Magical Realism

In the opening dedication of *Bougainvillea and Other Stories*, Chakraborty notes that his inspirations are the working and middle classes. Such sympathies fuel the aspiration of writers worldwide, including John Steinbeck in America and in France, Jean Genet. In 20th and 21st Century literature, the heroes tend to be common people who are portrayed in situations of their failures and shortcomings — and occasionally seen as resilient, hapless heroes. Working class gentlemen in literature run parallel to the soldiers of the Great Man Theory studied in history classes.

The difficulty presented in this collection of stories is the tediousness of translating texts into well-crafted versions of their originals. There are some noteworthy admissions, as in "Bougainvillea," when the language barrier is revealed for what it is. We have a character who isn't cosmopolitan enough to speak English well as do those acculturated to it. He candidly admits his English is good *enough* for

Calcutta. The reader is aware at this point that he or she is watching a man lie to himself, imagining a greater knowledge of English is a great knowledge. In translation, prose and verse alike are distinct in two languages. There often aren't words to depict certain meanings in the alternate language especially in the creative spontaneity of poetry. All translations are short of truth and actual word-for-word synthesis.

Translators are faced with the singular problem of being true to the original, knowing the limits of translation, and hence having to adapt the work to their own imaginations. Translators are forced to use poetic license to make a circle fit into a square. When all else fails, the best vehicle is one's own original thought. No translation will be complete. Phrasing is different in each language, characters are different, and even the sound of words are unique to each work. When moving a text from its original to a new place, some of the thought and feeling can be lost because the heart of each language is unique. Some languages are perhaps more romantic, or religious, and English (as we know it today) is perhaps a language best suited for contracts and business arrangements. In many ways, the language is upside down compared to others.

Yet we must admit the importance of language and translation. Seeing a work in letters in one's own tongue introduces you to new cultures and themes.

What many don't realize is how language creates the character of a people. There are languages in use that don't differentiate between genders. One language I read about was place and direction oriented, and the people who spoke it understood those things intuitively. Language is what we as humans use to convey and preserve signs, thoughts, attitudes, and manners. Words are vehicles that drive the spirit of a country. Poets seek to redefine culture using language's barriers and distinct patterns, and myth centralizes after a people's literary achievements are surveyed. For instance, the archeology of ancient Palestine would have no context without the literature of Scripture. Archaeological discoveries are compared and discussed, and myths surveyed for clues until a consensus (a guess based on sensible conclusions) is reached. Art tells the future who we are, where we went, and what of their own footing our deed was. The torch is passed and myth contains the mysteries of eternity. It is a meeting place between a nation and a nation's god. Pluralism encourages competition in culture — not cutthroat competition, but mutually beneficial exchange — and a transfer of ideas from one place to the next. Sometimes misunderstandings push you to boundaries when you may have dropped your knapsack sooner. Variety challenges our assumptions, awakens healthy doubts, and enriches our lives — diversity keeps things interesting, alive, and prevents cultural stagnation. Those who are pushed to the margins of a culture will embrace an outsider's viewin. Keep in mind *The Bible* was written by Hebrews, the bastard children of ancient Israel.

Common men and women are portrayed in this collection, sometimes in their discontents and at other times in their shortcomings. We also see how weighty their realities are as characters are assaulted with commercial images when they are down on their luck. Modern technology is shown throughout as a hindrance to communication and success, the very opposite of its intent. The average fellow is constantly frustrated, afraid, dejected, and lost spiritually. Civilization and its discontents irk and disenfranchise our noble characters in each story.

"Bougainvillea" is unique in that it seems to ascribe value to these sufferings. The protagonist is injured by a flowerless plant and decides this monstrosity should be destroyed. He is reminded by his family that the plant will show flowers someday and that it needs to be trimmed, not completely ripped asunder. The protagonist seems appalled and is reminded of his incompetence and petty grievances. The moral begins to unravel: this plant may prick you frequently but if tamed carefully, it won't prick you and in fact will grow beautiful flowers. This seems to remind us that it's our perception of things that make us failures to our own eyes. The metaphorical "pricks" are the sharp heartaches and damnations we face when we reach out into the world for employment, scholarship, or to achieve our goals, and instead face our own backsliding and inability to actualize our dreams.

I have often faced this trouble in my own life, and I am sure very few haven't. Each step in the ladder offers an opportunity to fall. Christian doctrine teaches that we are fallen creatures, but that in spite of our fallen nature we can be redeemed through Jesus Christ and his teachings — which are thought to stimulate new outlooks and help us forgive ourselves. Letting go of mistakes is the first step to moving forward again. You may not be a Christian (I myself am not), but you can't deny this powerful lesson.

One of the most provoking stories (other than "The Assassinator") is "Martyr's Column." The reason I single this story out is its mournful irony is deep. You may interpret the ideas differently. However, the strange mysticism of the plot awakens discreet thoughts and may engage you in self-discussion. This story is powerful.

Very symbolic! "The Assassinator" engages in a symbolism of cause and effect. Why people fight revolution and why desperation encourages discontent! This is a story of intrigue and importance. It portrays a sense of unjustified fear — something in the lurch — and the changing of pace only escalates the overall impression. The story is translated coherently and I assume accurately.

There is almost a dream-like hinge of climax, a sudden awakening, and a feeling of resolution at the end. You almost get a sense of refreshing news, that the previous lines were not real, that everything is fine, the story was a daydream.

Clearly the author is a sympathizer with humanity — a humanist, a traditionalist who recognizes the troubles of modern technology and commercialism, and a sincere and imaginative storyteller who can capture your mind as long as you are ensconced within his stories. Perhaps "ensconced" is not the right word. I'll let you, reader, choose your own word.

Dustin Pickering
May 8, 2016
Editor-in-Chief, Harbinger Asylum
Founder, Transcendent Zero Press, Texas

Acknowledgements

I'm grateful both to my publisher and translator for their painstaking effort in bringing out the collection of stories in the English language for the global readers.

I'm thankful to all the reviewers and critics for their overwhelming support and critical appreciation received by the original Bengali book, *Santiram-er Cha*.

Table of Contents

Bougainvillea

Sanjeeb feels like vomiting after he puffs at the cigarette for the second time. He fails to understand why he was feeling like that for the last couple of days. How many did he smoke since morning? A packet! May be. Sanjeeb now does not know what to do with the cigarette. Will he throw it away? Rubbish! If he has to vomit, be it so. Let all the cells of the body and the nerves that excite be thrown up. For the last few days Sanjeeb has been getting a sensation of his body becoming heavy. He has no clear understanding of the reason behind. Again at times he seems to understand the reason behind it. Like a shadowy-unclear death! However, Sanjeeb is absolutely aware of its certainty. Fear — fear of taking into account the difference between the profit and the loss you make if you live or die. Fear of the growing difference between your aspiration and unfulfilled desire.

The cell-phone is humming the old polyphonic tone. Oh! Impossible. Sanjeeb feels ashamed of pulling out this primitive phone while on the streets. While cell-phones have become a mobile music system nowadays, this pre-historic set, feels Sanjeeb, is really out of place. Amalendu has shown him a new set yesterday. It will cost four-thousand bucks. He told Sanjeeb that he would accept payment in installments. Sanjeeb has planned to pay five-hundred bucks every month for eight consecutive months. The tuition fee he gets at Shyampukur will take care of it. He will go there to give tuition today. While he was coming back *kakima* forced the money in his hand and said, "You need not come anymore. He has failed to understand the tuition you give. He learns absolutely nothing." Sanjeeb has been irregular this month. He was thinking today of making good the lost days next month. Let it be! Alas! He would not be able to buy the new phone he thought of. Amalendu will not accept the amount that he would probably save from other tuitions after he had provided for his family. After all, he has to look after his business! Sanjeeb is left with no choice, but he pulls out his ancient phone. Tired love is waiting for a response on the other side of the black and white screen.

"Are you through with your tuition?"

"Yes."

"I have been calling you since long. Why weren't you receiving my call?"

"I was talking to kakima after I had finished giving lessons."

"Did they pay your monthly fee?"

"Yes."

"Oh!! That's good news."

"Hmm!"

"What's the matter? Are you not well? Why aren't you speaking?"

"No. Just like that."

"Tell me, what's wrong?"

"Anyway, aren't we meeting tomorrow? Is it necessary to waste money on telephone calls?"

"Sanjeeb, you are not paying for the call."

"I don't feel like talking."

"Okay, fine!"

Sanjeeb did not wait for the last burst of emotion on the other side. He slipped the phone into his pocket. He fails to recollect when he threw away the cigarette. He just felt that his head was growing heavier.

2

"Ouch!" Sanjeeb felt a burning sensation on the skin of his left palm. He lifted his hand and saw in the light brown glow of the streetlight and found that underneath his skin blood has clotted in fine black and red speckles. Could anyone plant such thorny bush at the entrance? All crazy people! How many times had he not suggested that the tree be felled? No! Dad had bought if for only twelve rupees from Sealdah station, the "red bougainvillea." "Fucking bougainvillea will blossom! Rather, it will kill us in a few days!"

Sanjeeb generally is on his watch out when he enters home. He wants to gauge how heated the environment is inside. Almost every day, around this time, his parents engage in tumultuous stock taking. At times they end their debate staying within the limit of gentleness at midnight, but at times they unfairly cross the borderline.

"…It's not possible for me to run the household like this. If I spend, you will ask, where has all the money gone? Your son takes on me if the food tastes bad. I told you to visit the market once, and find out for yourself what it is like! But you will not do that. Instead you will immerse yourself in the newspaper since morning! You will then bathe and eat and leave for your office…"

This has been a simple equation for Sanjeeb's mother. To show a suspense account in her balance sheet after dragging Sanjeeb into it. He, quite annoyed, tapped on the door.

"Coming!"

Sanjeeb took his shoes off and all the while looked very grim. After placing the mobile, his spectacles and the five-hundred rupee note on the table he asked his mother,

"Give me a glass of water, ma. Do we have some Dettol in home?"

After giving him water to drink his mother asked,

"Apu, what is this money for?"

"Shyampukur tuition fee."

"So early in the month! Isn't it a premature payment?"

"I have lost the tuition."

"You have lost this too? Now how will I run the household? You spend half of what you bring on yourself."

"What do you mean by spending on myself? Are all the bus-owners my in-laws that they will take me to the interview venues free of cost?"

Without responding to Sanjeeb's arrogant reply his mother went to the other room.

"What happened?"

Sanjeeb knew it would now be his father's turn, but he answered patiently.

"He could not follow my classes, it seems."

"Won't you study yourself before going to take the class?"

"Baba, to give tuition to an eighth-grade student you need not study."

"Before you give notes it's important you study reference books. Students improve in the process and secure better marks."

"Whatever notes I give are sufficient. Do you practice accountancy every morning before you sit at office with its expenses?"

"Ma, did I not ask for Dettol?"

After changing his clothes, Sanjeeb brought water in a small jug and examined his wound. His mother placed a dusty vial of Dettol on the table and questioned,

"What has happened to your hand?"

"What will happen with the thorny shrub that has been planted at the entrance? It's the same old story every day. One day it would blossom! Will Nakul*da* not come to clear the bushes tomorrow? Just see, how I get it felled."

3

"Who would get down at the Howrah Station?"

Sanjeeb gets astonished whenever he sees this part of the city. Probably, the most tired city of the world. From morning to night the people tiredly bear the time, and stay busy. The exhausted officegoers cling on to the overcrowded buses — they fight … they compete. Tiredness oozes out of Sanjeeb's body into his handkerchief. For fifteen minutes the bus stood still before it rolled onto the Howrah Bridge! The conductor went on calling out for passengers. If you stand here you could spot an old church. Atop the church the Jesus stands with his hands spread trying to raise a storm of peace. His clothing flutters in the air. Do the tired passengers see this? Do they become calm? Sanjeeb feels like laughing. The person who had installed the statue had pulled a fast one. Peace!

Sanjeeb made sure that his cell-phone was in place. Before facing the interview board he switched off his phone; he didn't switch it on after that. Mou waits expectantly on days like these. Perhaps she thinks that the turn of new life has finally arrived. Sanjeeb knows how unbearable it is to carry the weight of such expectations. He took pity on himself. Shall he switch on the mobile now? Shall he put a definitive full stop on the thought process at the other end?

Sanjeeb looked out of the window to look at the statue of Jesus once again. The eyes of the statue were pointing towards Kolkata. One warm sunbeam had illuminated the smile on Jesus' face. That smile seems totally out of place on the way of this tiring journey.

The first caller after he switched on the mobile was Mou. Sanjeeb waited for a few seconds. He prepared the answers to the questions supposedly waiting at the other end.

"Sanjeeb! What's up?"

"They would inform me later."

"Oh! Where are you now?"

"Howrah Station."

"I am entering Sealdah. Would you come?"

"Where, at Sealdah?"

"Yes, at the coffee shop upstairs!"

Did Mou calculate before embarking on her journey? Sanjeeb was in two minds.

This coffee shop has been Mou's discovery. Sanjeeb did not even know that there was such a restaurant at the first floor of the Sealdah station. The crowd may not be enormous but the place stays busy throughout because of some long-distance travelers. At the entrance he spotted Mou sitting with a cup of tea. She ordered toast and tea the moment she spotted Sanjeeb. He needed the food badly. The rice he ate in the morning got digested in the 10.22 am Barrackpore local itself. Mou looked at her watch and asked,

"Don't you have any tuition to go to?"

"Yes, at 6 pm today. What is the time now?"

"Thirty two minutes passed four. What happened at the interview?

"I told you over the phone."

"What did you mean by they would inform?"

"The 'meaning' is easy, Mou; they will not hire me. I meant, I did not get the job."

"What went wrong?"

Sanjeeb in a patient tone requested the bearer who had come to give the toast to give a glass of water. Mou was watching Sanjeeb; her eyes did not bat. Sanjeeb turned his face at the other direction and replied,

"The same old story. Communication problem!"

"Oh! How many times did I not tell you to get admitted in the spoken-English class?"

"Look Mou, I did not clear the graduation for nothing! I agree that I'm weak in the English language by the American standard, but what I speak works well in Kolkata."

"Now that it is not working you should understand. Sanjeeb, time does not stand still. It's about a year now that we left college. I failed to get admission in the Masters. My father is not sitting idle, Sanjeeb."

"Okay Mou, you can also look out for a job. Why do you think that a man becomes eligible to marry a woman the moment he attains economic independence?"

"Sanjeeb, won't you suffer from an inferiority complex that your wife would earn to feed you?"

"No, I will not suffer."

"But, I will have problems even if you do not have. I will not be able to tell people in my society that my husband is unemployed."

Sanjeeb suddenly bursts into a laughter.

"Unemployed? What do you mean, Mou? I earn twenty-two-hundred rupees every month."

"Don't laugh, Sanjeeb; life needs financial stability."

"Mou, that is only possible on paper. Every material looks for stability. But, in reality it is impossible. At least for a worthless guy like me it is barely possible."

"Well, at least by now you have understood that you are good for nothing!"

"Yes, of course. That's why I feel that a good-for-something like you should not wait for a good-for-nothing like me. Egg your father on to do some good search for a suitable groom."

"What my father is supposed to do you need not advice at all. You tell me clearly what you want."

Mou looked straight at Sanjeeb, demanding an answer. Sanjeeb felt quite uncomfortable. He lowered his face below his chin and answered,

"I am telling you clearly, Mou, our relationship has become a thorn of a thorny shrub. I think we should stop here."

Mou listened to Sanjeeb attentively. Then she did her bag, went straight to the counter, cleared the bill, and left. Sanjeeb remained seated on his chair for sometime. There was still some tea left in his cup.

4

Sanjeeb's sleep was broken by the sound of Nakul*da*'s sickle working on the bushes that grew underneath the window. Today he had no tuition to go to, so he wanted to wake up late. Nakul*da* was supposed to come yesterday but could not. Sanjeeb loosened one corner of the mosquito net and came out of it. Nakul*da* generally keeps his words. He catches the first train to their place. He returns to his home in the afternoon. He comes once in a month. Sanjeeb's mother gets some important work done by him; at times even the work of a mason.

"There is a *Kalmegh* plant there, mind you. Do not uproot it."

Sanjeeb's father was protecting his favorite plant standing on the door with a newspaper in his hands. Otherwise his father hardly has any interest in such things as these. Even when this house was built he hardly took any interest other than taking stock of some minor anomaly in the accounts done by Sanjeeb. Sanjeeb walked past his father and stood on the lower stairs to the garden.

"Nakul*da*, come here at first!"

"Jai Nitai. Here I come. How are you doing?"

"Fine. Just cut this tree off!"

"Which one? Oh! Why would you fell the lady bougainvillea? How beautifully it would blossom!"

"No need of flowers. Every day I get pricks and will perhaps die one day because of that."

"No, no! Do not fell that tree, Nakul." Sanjeeb's father issued a firm order.

"Come on, who would plant a bushy shrub like that at the entrance?"

"Nothing much would matter. Wait, a little bit of trimming would work."

Father issued his diktat. He went back abed with his newspaper.

"Just trimming would work! No, Nakul*da*, you will have to fell that tree."

"Babu has told the right thing. You get pricked, so let's trim the tree a bit. Do you realize what beautiful flowers will blossom once this tree grows to its full?"

"Have mercy, *Nakul*da. This daily assault cannot be tolerated anymore!"

"Do you know why it pricks you every day?"

"I need not know! Ma, may I have some tea?"

"It tells you repeatedly to take care of it." Nakul continues, "Dadababu, this tree tells you: "When I grow up I will give you shade, I will look great, so take care of me.""

Sanjeeb showed his annoyance.

"Just keep quite. Do not eat my head in the morning. Fell that tree immediately."

"You will cut the tree only because it pricks you! Look many things in our lives give us pricks, do we cut and throw out all those things?"

5

Sanjeeb has not seen Mou this way for a very long time. The song Mou is now singing, she has not sung for many days now. This song appears to be very familiar … extremely familiar. But he fails to recollect the song. Mou is dancing in joy. Perhaps it is Holi today. Mou has smeared herself in different colors. Once Mou smeared Sanjeeb with colors during Holi and he looked like a ghost. Even today Mou has put all the colors on her. But what the colors are Sanjeeb fails to figure out. They are all in black and white. Sanjeeb feels like touching Mou, but he fails to understand how far he is from her. Is it quite a distance? But why? Why is Mou so far away? She is slowly disappearing in the crowd. Some trees are growing around her ... those are making her disappear amidst them. The trees are growing fast and Sanjeeb tries to reach out to Mou even faster! The trees are thorny, bushy. As those were in black and white he fails to understand if these were bougainvillea! But these have no flowers. Only thorns on them. The faster Sanjeeb moves, the thorns prick him all the more and pierces his body. The pricks burned Sanjeeb. The black blood clotted all over his skin and made his body wet ... his pillow, bed and bed-sheet have become moist because of his sweat.

Today it is really humid, so humid that the air from the ceiling fan is not entering the mosquito net. Sanjeeb sets the table-fan in order in the darkness itself and switched it on. The dull lights shine in the darkness on the street. The entire lane is deserted. Yet Sanjeeb has a feeling that someone will go away now; will go away smeared in colors.

6

"How are you, Sanjeeb?"

The clouds have gathered in the sky after quite a while. Cool breeze was blowing since evening. Perhaps it will rain, or it has rained somewhere!

"How are you? Why did you call me up all of a sudden?"

"Just like that. Could you come to that coffee shop at Sealdah, Mou?"

"Why?"

"I felt like seeing you once."

The other side was silent. Sanjeeb went on,

"I have enrolled in the spoken-English class, Mou."

"Not today, Sanjeeb, some other day. Go back home, soon it will rain."

The speed of the cool breeze was fast increasing; a storm will occur soon. Rain caught him as he entered the street leading to his home. He will have to return to his home fast. This rain gives Sanjeeb a burning sensation on his skin. The side from which these clouds came to shower, there they have stopped playing with colors. All the bougainvillea there stay awake expectantly for their flowers to blossom. There stands hidden the gloom that mixes in the rain.

Sanjeeb's shirt has almost got drenched in the rain. Sanjeeb pushed the gate in a bid to reach the door fast. His shirt got caught in the thorn of bougainvillea. It was actually a new shirt and he failed to get it released. The rain burnt the wounds in his whole body. An unbearable sense of burning! Is it when you are put off that you feel this burning sensation? Mou is put off, the bougainvillea is put off!

Sanjeeb tried to get his shirt released with a fierce tug; the shirt got torn near the pocket in the process, but he failed to get rid of the thorn. In the meanwhile, the rain had become quite heavy. Suddenly Sanjeeb liked standing in the rain. For how many days he had not got drenched in rain like this? For how many days Mou had not clung to the end of his shirt like a thorn and said, "Wait for some more time, please!"?

For how long the gloom has not been washed away by tears like this…

The City in Winter

The cellphone beeped. Rwitabrata was forced to leave the bed. No one but the office people would send an SMS so early in the morning. Two urgent accounts of Shaw Garments got registered with them yesterday. The delivery would have to be done by today. The two mechanics were supposed to come in the morning and take the delivery. The office keys were with Tanmoy. Being a local guy he used to travel on cycle. Rwitabrata would reach office early today. A check given by the dealer has not been realized even now. He will have to go to the bank in the first hours of the day.

Rwitabrata tried to guess what the message could be. Did the mechanics fail to arrive on time? They were supposed to do the major portion of the work before the counters of the Shaw's opened. No work could be done once the counters opened. For this Tanmoy had dug the wall two days before. They repeatedly requested Rwitabrata over telephone, "Dada, you will have to ensure that the job gets done by the morning." He had assured them. If the work did not get completed by this morning, he would have to go to the office tomorrow, a Sunday. There was only a day off in a week. If the mechanics failed to turn up today there would be no holiday. Rwitabrata was too disgusted to even touch the phone. He unplugged the charger, opened the door of his bedroom and went back to his bed. It was the expected time when his mother would come out of the bathroom and make his bed. His father must have left for the bazar by now. His mother entered the room shuffling the clean sari that was to be worn in the morning. A pair of bronze-bangles and the two other holy bangles struck each other giving birth to a clinking sound. She grumbled as she was untying the mosquito net.

"On the other days … when I say, wake up early in the morning, see someone is plucking the flowers away, and I get nothing for the daily puja, then you wouldn't. But see, today…"

"What happened again?" Rwitabrata asked irritated.

"What's to happen? Please, get up and release the bed."

Rwitabrata left the bed. Dad must have been waiting today to speak to the boy who delivers newspaper. A story was being played out in the home for the last two days. Dad used to give the payment of the monthly newspaper bill to Paltu, but he has usurped the last month's payment entirely. Nitai*da* was able to spot the fraud when he came for collecting the payment on Monday. Rwitabrata told his father to opt for the combo offer for many a time. By opting for that offer one would get two newspapers both in the English and Bengali languages on a discounted rate. "You make the payment directly to the company through an account payee check. There isn't any hassle," he urged. Rwitabrata had even got him the application form, but his father would indulge in the same old problem!

"Who would read an English paper at home?" His father never failed to put forward his irrefutable logic. "Okay, if you don't read you can stock the papers for some months and sell them later," Rwitabrata had suggested.

Rwitabrata came back from the washroom and opened his shaving kit. His mother placed the morning cup of tea on the table and hurriedly left. The mobile phone that lay beside the cup reminded him of the unread SMS as it beeped again, but this time it was in a reminder tone. Rwitabrata almost forgot about the SMS. His mind cringed as he remembered it. If the godforsaken mechanics failed to turn up this morning Animesh*da* would raise a hell. And he always had one dialogue up on his lips if anything went wrong, "What for I am paying you handsome salaries?" Rwitabrata did not like it a bit. Let it be! Rwitabrata was disgusted with himself. Why was he thinking so much in the morning? Even Tanmoy might have sent the SMS after sending the mechanics to work.

Rwitabrata picked up the mobile. No it's not Tanmoy. It's from an unknown number. The moment he pressed the read button the black digital letters appeared on screen.

"Let your birthday arrive time and again, wrapped in the veil of winter. Happy Birthday!"

2

"Dada, try and go inside, I am hanging outside the train."

Two more people shouted from outside the train compartment.

"Oh God! They are hanging. Why don't you push your way inside, O' dada?"

No visible reaction could be spotted inside the compartment. Rwitabrata tilted towards his right and stood slanted. He waited. This crowd pressure will not ebb before the train reaches Dum Dum. No sooner than the train had left the station the Dum Dum bound passengers started to push and jostle. Someone elbowed Rwitabrata's tummy. Had it been on any other day he would have abused the person like hell. But today he failed to get angry. He just raised his voice and said, "Dada, watch your steps as you push your way out of the compartment."

No one responded. Rwitabrata had been engulfed by a unique curiosity mixed with joy today. He really did not remember his birthday. The most amazing thing was whose number this could have been who had remembered and made him remember that today was his birthday! He responded thanking the sender but the reply he got was equally evasive.

"I thank God."

"Had He not sent you in the earth, I could not have met you ever."

"Just think how much I would have missed out on!"

That such an expectation of getting something or other might be entwined with his birth. Rwitabrata just could not think anymore. He replied—

"What do you mean? Do I know you?"

A reply to his message was yet to arrive. Rwitabrata in the meanwhile did some mental calculation. The main outcome of that calculation was that he would have to wait. Wait begets sweet results.

The crowd pressure increased as the train was approaching Dum Dum. Ouch! A booted leg had trampled Rwitabrata's. The people, like water flowing out of a breached dam, poured into the Dum Dum station. For some reason many people also boarded the train at the Dum Dum station. Rwitabrata began to move in the crowd, otherwise he would not be able to get down at the Bidhannagar station. His hands were aching, but there wasn't any way that he could bring them down. Suddenly something moved along his right thigh, he felt. Rwitabrata could not know for sure, his legs had lost their senses after standing for long in the same posture. Did some hand enter his pocket? He became conscious. No, his cellphone vibrated perhaps. Was that an incoming call? No, the phone vibrated only for a short while. What made the phone vibrate? Rwitabrata's hair stood.

He ejected out of the station the moment the train reached Bidhannagar. He evaded the rush of the people and stood by the side of the railings. He pulled out the mobile from his pocket. "Yes! It's an SMS."

"I know you very well. But could you manage to recognize me?"

"Okay, let's play a game. I will give you three clues."

"If you recognize me … fine; but, if you fail, you will never get me. Please try and understand."

The train tracks suddenly left the ground and began to float in the air. Rwitabrata looked at a distance. Slowly everything, the bazar, the black road, the auto-rickshaws … were flying past him! The black road of the platform was covered by green grasses. Even in this December-winter the trees had red and blue flowers on them. The mundane shops on both side of the street had transformed into ice-cream parlors. Rwitabrata bought a cigarette. He wanted to buy an expensive one, but there were twelve days left for the month to end.

The monotonous road that led to Gouribari from the station had today been filled with mystery. For how many days, he did not correctly remember, Rwitabrata had not felt this pleasure shrouded in mystery. Almost three-and-one-half year. Rwitabrata rummaged through his gloom to fish out this calculation. Before then he was unaware of the fact that there was someone who could weave mystery even better than Feluda's mystery-net. So, Rwitabrata named her Spider. Jinia had giggled when she heard the name for the first time from him.

"The idea is brilliant though! Hollywood would lap it up. After Spiderman now it would be Spiderwoman. But, there is a problem!"

Rwitabrata looked at her curiously.

"You cannot be named as the creator of the idea."

"Why?"

"Because someone else has also told me this before."

"Who?"

"I won't tell."

"Please, Jinia!"

"No."

"Okay, tell me whether it was a he or a she."

"Hmm! A he, of course."

"Who?"

"Didn't I tell you that I will not say?"

"Please, please, and please…"

"You know him but."

"Who?"

"He is a bit smarter than you and even a bit tougher. Guess who that may be. If you guess correctly I will kiss you on three consecutive days, but if you fail I will not meet you for a week!"

Rwitabrata was in deep thoughts. Not with the name but with these seven days.

"Poor guy, you have failed miserably. You will not see me for seven days … and the answer is you. Oh God! Only you told me a few minutes before."

Jinia began to smile. A bus arrived and Jinia waived at it. A few people disembarked the moment the bus came to a standstill. Before boarding the bus Jinia brought her face close to Rwitabrata's ear and said, "You become even smarter when you get angry, trust me!"

Rwitabrata, like a fool, observed the bus leave. Seven days. 168 hours. 42 classes. Some crores of moments. He alone will have to tackle all Jinia's mysteries. In the joints friends pulled his leg. He remarked on, "He who has been rejected as a boyfriend twice only knows what it takes to have a steady girlfriend."

Even a Byomkesh or a Feluda did not have to solve in their whole lives even two percent of the mysteries that hit Rwitabrata in that one night.

3

"My favorite color is black."

Rwitabrata failed to remember whether he had seen Jinia in black. In spite of this he tried to close his eyes and think. No. Rwitabrata did not see her wear anything black apart from a dupatta of that color. In Rwitabrata's dream Jinia kept on returning in a dress that had sky-blue as its base color with white flowers printed on it. Her hair had a unique smell to it. Tinku*da*'s horrible tea shop would turn into a posh café, Barista, if Jinia could be seen at the balcony of her house. But black! No, the sky did never become overcast in those days, and the streetlights flooded the roads with moonlight every night. True, this was a very misleading clue! To be honest, Rwitabrata had no reason to know the answer to this question as he had never gifted Jinia any dress ever. He took her to the cinema only once. Bhansali's *Black*. Jinia did not like it at all, "The name itself smacks of something dead! The movie itself is a nag. Rubbish, total wastage of time."

Rwitabrata found himself guilty.

"Well, did you like the movie?"

Rwitabrata fell in trouble; he was not able tell her the truth.

"Are you asking me? I also did not like it, barring Rani Mukherjee!"

"I knew it."

Jinia jumped in joy, as if she had solved a long-filed case with an answer to just one question.

"Tell me one thing. Do you write poetry?"

Rwitabrata shuddered, "No, not at all … never!"

Rwitabrata became sure that the first clue did not point to Jinia.

"Rwitabrata*da*, your phone."

Rwitabrata's trance got dissolved. Tanmoy had placed the receiver on the table. Rwitabrata picked it up.

"Hello!"

"Rwitabrata, Swaroop here".

"Yes Sir, tell me."

"Where is Animesh?"

"Dada is out of the office. Do I need to tell him anything?"

"What would you say? You people forget us after taking the delivery. Now it is a fortnight that he has not paid a single penny. He promises big when an urgent delivery is required. But at the time of payment, all sorts of … do ask him for how long will he cheat people like this? I will also see how henceforth he receives urgent delivery without paying for the goods. I will stop all his dealers from doing so."

Rwitabrata felt annoyed. This has been a daily problem.

"Didn't you try his cellphone?

"Rubbish! The bastard had disconnected the line and switched his phone off. And now he is making you all receive the phone in the office."

"Believe me, Dada is really not in the office."

"Come on! What fucking place he could go to at noon? Listen bro, I'm into the business for a considerable period of time and I have become a father of two sons. Don't try to teach me."

"Dada has got another number. Please note it down. Have a talk with him."

Rwitabrata placed the receiver down with a bang. Tanmoy gave a sly smile.

"Wasn't it Swaroop*da*?"

Yes.

Rwitabrata went back to his table.

"You gave him Animesh*da's* private number!"

"Why won't I? Why should I be abused for nothing? Our bank account is sufficiently funded, so why would one delay the payment?"

"The bastard is a miser!"

It was Tanmoy's way of christening Animesh. What other adjective can be used for a man who cheats on the monthly salary of his employee? Tanmoy would get two-thousand-and-seven-hundred bucks as opposed to three-thousand bucks as it was fixed at the time of his appointment.

"Tanmoy, is the work at the Shaw's done? Could you inquire?"

"No, the mechanics are supposed to return here in the office; they are expecting a payment that is overdue."

"Today no payment can be done. Dada has not left behind any cash for disbursement."

Rwitabrata quickly checked the mobile phone kept on the table. "Did Jinia like black at all?" The same question kept surfacing on his mind as he looked at the black cabinet of his office computer. No, Jinia did never like black. Else how could the film that made Rwitabrata twice remove his glasses to wipe his tears, become a nag for her? Impossible, it could never be Jinia.

But a person's liking and disliking could change over a period of three years. Could they not? But, it was possible so far as Jinia was concerned. Vanilla was the flavor that Jinia liked among ice-creams. One day when he ordered vanilla at the Tasty, she objected,

"No, I will not take vanilla today. I'll go for chocolate."

"How come? But vanilla is your favorite."

"No, I changed it only yesterday!"

Rwitabrata looked at Jinia bewildered. As it was, chocolate was costlier by two rupees; and then if there was no cup available, a cone would be costlier at least by six or seven rupees. Could a person's preference change so fast?

"Dada, I am going out for lunch. Ask the mechanics to wait when they come."

Tanmoy brought out his cycle. Rwitabrata urged Tanmoy once—

"Tanmoy, could you order a cup of tea for me on your way?"

The year-end was approaching closer. One needed to settle the accounts fast during this time of the year. Rwitabrata had paid a hefty price for his unkempt life. Last year Animesh took one-thousand rupees to fuel his car without signing a voucher. He completely denied that after three months when the accounts were being done.

"I have never taken money to fill my car from your cash, Rwitabrata. Apply your mind a bit more as you work. If I deduct all these from your salary at the end of the month what all will you eat?"

Animesh did not wait even for a while. He went back to his cabin and disappeared. Rwitabrata looked at the calendar and anxiously searched for his next salary date.

The cell-phone kept on the table was vibrating. Again there was an SMS. It was blank. A blank SMS! Rwitabrata was amused. He began to scroll. He knew there was something at the end. He was right, the right hand side of the display screen showed: "Second clue." Immediately he brought the number to dial. It began to ring at the other end. He felt a sudden surge of blood flow within. It went on ringing followed by a recorded voice message, "Dialed number is busy. Please try after sometime." Rwitabrata calmed himself down at once. He kept the mobile down on the table and went back to his deep thoughts.

Tanmoy came back to the office, but Rwitabrata failed to get back to the real world; he kept floating in Jinia's flower-printed sky.

"What does this mean?"

Jinia smiled in response. She had sent a blank SMS at twelve in the night the other day. Jinia at this odd hour! Rwitabrata dialed Jinia's number at once. She declined the call. Three consecutive trials. What a problem! "Jinia should at least receive the call." The next day Rwitabrata bunked two classes and finally could catch Jinia at the third floor after her class was over.

"Tell me, what does it mean?"

"Just like that. I was bothering you a bit."

There was an irritating noise coming out of something. Rwitabrata looked around him. Tanmoy was not at his table, he was in Animesh*da*'s cabin.

"Animesh*da* has returned". As he was bringing his eyes back on his table the mobile phone caught his eyes again. There was yet another SMS waiting to be read by Rwitabrata.

"I'm in office. Please call me after 8 pm."

4

"Hello!"

"Please come to my cabin once."

Rwitabrata got up. Tanmoy gave a smile with lips pressed together. He cut a joke about Animesh using his eyes. Animesh was seated at his desk with bills scattered all over the table. He raised his eyes the moment Rwitabrata entered his cabin.

"Did you go to the bank?"

"Yes."

Rwitabrata passed on the pass-book to Animesh.

"I have made it up-to-date."

Animesh ran his eyes through the last leaf of the book.

"The work at the Shaw's has been completed. The two mechanics will come here anytime. Give them some payment today."

"But dada, I have no cash with me."

Animesh fished out two notes of rupees five hundred each and placed those on the table.

"Pay them and inform them that the rest will be given later."

Rwitabrata nodded his head and picked up the notes.

"Did Swaroop call?"

"Yes."

"Who had given him the number of my residence?"

"I gave him."

Animesh angrily looked at Rwitabrata,

"Who asked you to give him my private number?"

"He called up and was abusing you."

"But for that you will give him the number? You have not learned to handle such situations even now. And listen, this is a private firm, not a government office; if you want to stay here go and pick up the habit of enduring abuses."

"I am not accustomed to abuses, dada." Rwitabrata's jaws stiffened.

"Come to this office tomorrow only if you would make it a practice to hear abuses; if you don't agree there is no need to come here again!" Animesh looked straight at him.

Rwitabrata did not wait for any more words. He came back to his table. He sat in a relaxed way. He was feeling glad. A joy of freedom ... the cell-phone vibrated again. He brought out the mobile.

"Third clue."

"Among the four days of the Durga Puja, the Saptami is my favorite."

Rwitabrata's body loosened up. Three and a half years ago even he felt that Saptami was his favorite. Tukai had conveyed him the message in the morning: "Jinia*di* has asked you to wait for her here, in front of Tinku*da's* tea shop in the evening."

Jinia was Tukai's private tutor. Rwitabrata jumped in joy. Immediately Bappa announced, "Today Vhochka will pay for our tea."

On any other day Bappa would have received three or four of Ritwabrata's choicest slangs for calling him Vhochka.

"But I will not pay for the cigarettes and I will not pay for Raja's tea."

Raja smiled, he did not utter a word. The bastard brought all the wrong information from all the places. Yesterday, as Raja told Rwitabrata, he had seen Jinia walking down the street with Deepabrata at Hedua. Bappa brought his nose close to Raja's mouth, smelled it once and twice, and said,

"O' boy! Are you on marijuana these days?" Raja laughed out loud.

Rwitabrata spent the afternoon in his home and came to Tinku*da*'s tea shop in the evening.

"Oh Raja! Come, sit and have some tea."

Rwitabrata was surprised a bit. He looked at his wrist watch. There was still one-and-a-half hour to go before the clock would strike six. Anyway, he could spend the time gossiping with his friends.

"Raja, would you not go anywhere today?"

"No."

Raja smiled. Rwitabrata was a bit annoyed. Might be without a reason, but he did get annoyed. Raja had started it since yesterday. Last evening he suddenly said,

"Rwitabrata, where is Jinia?

"Why?"

"Come on, tell me!"

"I do not know. She told me that she would go to Howrah station to receive her father. Her father would return from Guwahati today. He is returning for good this time."

"What is the matter Raja?"

"Did I see something wrong then? I thought I saw Jinia at Hedua today with Deepabrata."

As if Rwitabrata was hit by a Tsunami. "Jinia!" He had seen Jinia come to the college with Deepabrata on many days. Deepabrata stayed in the same locality as that of Jinia. He was Jinia's elder brother's friend. "For this if we meet on the road or in the bus we come together to the college. There is nothing between us, come on!" Irritated Jinia had said this when Rwitabrata asked about Deepabrata. Rwitabrata let the matter rest there. But then, why did she tell a lie today?

Rwitabrata brought out the phone and called Jinia. It began to ring at the other end. Once, twice, thrice… "Dialed number is busy. Please…" Rwitabrata tried the number twice more, but to no avail. Jinia repeatedly declined the calls. Finally, Rwitabrata got an SMS: "I am busy; call me after 8 pm."

Rwitabrata must have called twelve hundred times up to twelve noon the next day. Jinia's cell-phone had been kept off. At last Tukai called up to inform. Rwitabrata thought, "One must understand that one has to go through both easy and uneasy times."

Rwitabrata once again looked at his watch. It was 8.30 pm. Raja ordered yet another cup of tea. Other friends did not join them in their evening adda, everyone had some program to attend to.

"May I now call her up once?"

"Please do."

Raja offered a cup of tea to Rwitabrata.

"Can I use your phone?"

Raja gave him the phone. Jinia could not be reached as her phone had been kept switched off.

"Do one thing. Call up Tukai to confirm the exact time Jinia had said."

"This is a good idea." Rwitabrata called up Tukai.

"Jinia*di* may not go there today. She would go to some other place."

"Where would she go?"
"I'm not sure, she might accompany Deepabratada as they have booked a cab today."

Rwitabrata lowered the phone on the bench itself. The entire stretch of the road as long as it could be seen became blurred. Was it raining?

"Dada, may I come in?"

"Please."

"Here is the money. The mechanics have not come today. I have prepared their payment receipts, you can give them the money tomorrow."

"What do you mean by give them?"

"I may not come to the office tomorrow."

"Why?"

"I want to give it a thought. I want to realize whether I would be able to continue my job only to get abused!"

5

It would take ten minutes to reach the Bidhannagar station if one would take a bus. It would take half-an-hour by walking. Rwitabrata decided to save the bus fare. He lit a cigarette as he was walking up to the Gouribari Bridge. Five minutes left to 8 pm. He felt relaxed, as if he could fly in the sky if he would become a bit lighter.

He pulled out his mobile as he threw the cigarette butt in the canal below. He dialed the number. The name got displayed on the screen: "Mysterious." Beep … beep… It was really cold today. His fingers were losing the sense of touch slowly. Ring… ring … ring…

"Good evening, Sir!"

"Hello!"

"Yes Sir, how can I help you?"

"Actually since morning I have received a few SMSs from your number. "Who has sent them, do you have a clue?"

"Would you kindly tell me your name, please?"

"Rwitabrata Sen."

"And your phone number?"

"Nine three…"

"I got it, Sir. Today is your birthday. One of your friends has sent the SMSs to give you a pleasant surprise. There were three clues…"

"What is the name of my friend?"

"Sir, this is a secret. You have up until twelve at night; if you could name the person you would win from us a…" Rwitabrata disconnected the call. The winter seemed to disappear by the time he came off the bridge. Sweat accumulated on his ear lobes, Rwitabrata looked at the sky. "Has the winter departed for sure?" But, the billboards were not telling that. "Bask in winter … with us," the entire advertisement was wrapped in red and blue sweaters. Rwitabrata smiled at himself. The advertisement of sweaters was absolutely out of sync with this warm city!

Note: Feluda and Byomkesh are two private investigators — famous fictional characters of Bengali literature. They have been created by Satyajit Ray and Sharadindu Bandyopadhyay respectively. Sanjay Leela Bhansali is a mainstream Bollywood director and *Black* has been his award-winning movie.

Martyrs' Column

The ripple of a quake ran through Subodh's entire body! A cup of tea that he was holding in his right hand spilled and fell on his pajama.

"Uff!"

Subodh groaned. Ujjala stopped as she was leaving the room.

"What has happened?"

"Nothing! The tea spilled onto my legs."

Subodh quickly took control of himself. He kept the turned-in newspaper on the table.

"Consult the doctor now. I think you too have contracted a nerve-related disease. The way your hands shake these days, and quit smoking, please."

"Yeah, I am contemplating on quitting cigarettes."

"You will die contemplating." Disgusted Ujjala went to the kitchen. She stays really busy at this hour of the morning. Kona will leave for college. She has to cook rice and dal now. Subodh, who survives on pension, has yet to show the luxury of appointing a cook. Subodh leaves for the local market as per the needs after scanning the entire newspaper.

He has made it a practice to go to the market well past morning, so he can save a bit. The vendors, in order to catch the up Hansnabad or Bongaon local, sell the vegetables at low rates and leave around this time.

Today Subodh did not go through the front page today. He read the knee-pain story of Sania Mirza on the last page. On the bottom of the page there was a big advertisement carrying the photograph of a flat. "Now a slice of Santiniketan in Kolkata!" Subodh had built this home some eighteen years ago. Arindam, his son, was eleven-year-old then. Kona was only two-and-a-half-year-old. Along with two bed rooms, a kitchen, a puja room, a bathroom and a small verandah the home measured about nine-hundred-seventy-five square feet. Subodh did not get any of his father's property. With the savings he made from the salary that he was paid in his quasi-government job and adding to it the property that Ujjala got from her parents, he had constructed this house, and he named it "Bosot Bati" (Residential Abode). Subodh's favorite place in this house was the verandah. He relaxes on the cane chair he bought from North Bengal and shuffled through the old books. Not that he meticulously reads them; he carefully watches the alley in front of the verandah while sitting there. Unknown people who walk through this quite hamlet, sales men, mad men, little boys and girls returning from their schools — he sees all of them. Subodh does not know why he keeps watching them, but he has started to believe that he enjoys the idleness of his superannuated life sitting in this verandah. He does not indulge in such activities as morning or evening walk, barring his visit to the bazar. In the evenings Ujjala sits on the bed with stretched legs and watchesdaily soaps. Kona joins her and watches a couple of those after returning from her college. Subodh sits in the lightless verandah and listens to their conversation, making mental images in the process. He used to enjoy this a lot before, but now he has lost interest in it. The same thing gets repeated every half-an-hour.

"Instead of sitting like a dumb you could walk a bit in the morning and evening, can't you?" Subodh does not reply to Ujjala's message. In response he gets up, goesto his small dark room and tries to sleep. Ujjala lowers the volume of the television set as it strikes nine in the evening. Kona sits to study. Ujjala starts cooking rice at quarter to ten and warms the already cooked foods. Around 11pm both Ujjala and Subodh goes to bed after finishing their dinner while Kona goes back to studies.

Today he did not spend much time in the bazaar. The sun was beating down hard. He felt tired. He evaded the known tea stalls pretending to be in a hurry. By now, courtesy Subir*da*, everyone must have read the news. Subir*da* has a sharp memory. He has a knack to remember everyone's names, even the names of their sons after hearing them only once. He must have taken the news to the town by now after reading it. A retired employee of the central government, Subir*da*, is adept in doing such things. He only*is* the central figure behind the two get-togethers in the morning and evening, and during this period of gigantic leisure. In the morning it is the tea shop of Laltu between 10 amto11.30 am and during the evening it is the great card enthusiasts' congregation in the club house of Mitali Sangha. On his way to the bazaar, responding to the call of this very Subir*da*, Subodh stands for a while and indulges in gossips. He got acquainted with Subir ages ago in the local train. That acquaintance limps ahead even today in these times of leisure.

Someone has parked a car in a very awkward way in front of the lane. Mindless people! As Subodh entered the verandah of his house, disgusted, he was taken aback by the several pairs of shoes that lay there. The moment Ujjala spotted Subodh, she came forward and said in a suppressed voice,

"I do not know who all have come to meet you. I have asked them to sit in the room. Go and see."

Subodh entered the room. In all there were five unknown men. They were minutely scrutinizing the room. Everyone was neatly dressed. They were in formal dress with their shirts tucked in. They were all clean shaved. One had a thick moustache. Spotting

Subodh through the gap of his rimless specks he stood up to greet Subodh with folded hands.

"Namaskar, you are Subodh Bhattacharya?"

"Namaskar."

Bewildered Subodh answered.

"Please be seated. I am Nirmal Bagchi. They are Tapas, Swapan, K P Pandey and there he is Swarnamoy."

Everyone greeted Subodh but in a stern way. Subodh felt uneasy. Five pair of eyes were probing him closely. Subodh was more surprised to see Prajesh, who handed over five glasses of water that he brought from the kitchen to five of them. Prajesh was known as the "political-cum-social worker" of the area. But, why was he here with these people? Prajesh placed the tray in which he carried the glasses atop the cupboard and approached Subodh.

"Uncle, you know me, I guess."

Subodh nodded.

"These people want to talk to you. Please co-operate with them. Let's begin."

Subodh failed to realize what Prajesh meant. Co-operate about what?

"Have you read today's newspaper?"

NirmalBagchi began after taking a sip from the glass. Subodh slumped sat on the bed.

"Please come down. We are special officers of CID from Bhawani Bhavan."

The entire structure of Subodh swayed as if he were in space.

"A dead body was found yesterday in the jungles near Shalbani. I mean, during last night's regular patrol the Maoists fired at the police jeep, and when the forces retaliated they retreated. Then while conducting the search in the morning the body was found. Investigation says, the body is that of a Maoist, named Arindam Bhattacharya."

"Impossible."

Subodh groaned.

"Relax, Mr. Bhattacharya. We have found this voter's identity card with the body. Is this your son's photograph."

Subodh raised his head from his trembling body and saw the photograph.

"Yes! He is my son."

Subodh has tied all his nerves tightly in terrible fear and grief since he has read the report that did not carry any photograph in the morning. By now it has accumulated as vapor in his eyes. Bang! Subodh looked at the direction of the kitchen from where the noise came. Ujjala lay in the ground.

2

"There has been two sutures. Blood pressure is a bit high, but there is nothing to worry about. I have given her sleeping pills; she will feel better after she sleeps through the afternoon. Get the medicines, please. Has Kona come?"

"She is on her way. I did call her."

Subodh opened the gate in the verandah.

"Uncle, I know these words will sound like consolation, but I cannot even think that Arindam can do something like this. I saw the news in the morning, but…"

Subodh listened with his head lowered. He slipped into his chappal, as he listened; descended the stairs with Dr. Sen, but did not reply.

"Such a bright chap! Actually politics ruined their brains. They are on the prowl in the good universities to brainwash them. Whatever it is, uncle, now you have to be steady."

"Yes, I am."

Dr. Sen left.

During the fifth semester at the Jadavpur University Arindam came to know Dr. Sen who had then just begun to treat patients at the Seva Medical Hall. That evening Kona's temperature suddenly soared. Madhyamik, the board exam, was just around the corner; it was then… Ujjala on the other hand was determined to take Kona to Dr. Debnath. Subodh tried to reason with her, but Ujjala was adamant; she would consult no one other than the house physician. Arindam reasoned that during emergency everyone would become a house physician. He took Kona to Dr. Sen against all opposition. After Dr. Debnath passed away, Dr. Sen became the house physician of this "Residential Abode." He was a young man. He easily became friends with Arindam. They chatted sometimes when Dr. Sen used to come on periodical check-ups. Sometimes they discussed history, sometimes political history. Subodh at times used to get amazed at the depth and clarity of these two young men. One day the two had an engrossing discussion on history of medical science. Arindam, on that day, presented the topic with extreme logical coherence. Sen had a few "yes," "rightly said," and a few sighs for the answers. Even Subodh was mesmerized by the logical presentation of the transformation of the basic needs of human beings into commercial commodity. Even he had failed to realize all these that way until such an old age.

It is true how less a man understands in his entire life.

The doorbell rang twice. Subodh, after spending half-an-hour at noon, managed to put up a thick plastic screen on the grills of the verandah. The verandah appeared a little dark now. It appeared to Subodh that evening had suddenly set in.

The doorbell rang again. Subodh quickly got up and opened the door. Kona. Her entire face had darkened because of sweat and dust of the road. Subodh believed that Kona while passing through the localities before she reached home had shed a drop or two for her elder brother who had gone missing three years ago. Her eyes had become red and it could be seen in spite of her light grey glasses. A few strands of unoiled hair like the hood of a snake danced in the air near her forehead. The bag that was hanging from Kona's shoulders fell in front of the door. Instead of taking care of the slipping dupatta she dived on Subodh's chest,

"Baba, dada is really no more?"

"Dada, are you home?"

There was a power cut for almost an hour now. Subodh has gained much experience in the fast few hours. He has tackled at least four journalists. Nirmal Bagchi has repeatedly said, "Don't tell anything to the journalists. We would do that if needed." Kona is with her mother for hours at a stretch. Ujjalla has just taken a few spoons of rice and soup. Kona leaves Ujjala's room and informs Subodh, "Someone is calling you. Just see." Subodh is standing in the darkness and through the open window of the kitchen he is watching the buildings that has come up in the betel nut garden behind the garden of the Basak. Even some seven years ago around this time darkness would descend on that garden and a couple of jackals after being chased by the dogs would take shelter in the Basak's garden. It was Arindam and his friends who cleared a portion of the garden and played cricket there and Ujjala would stand at this window and call out,

"Babai, aren't you through with your game?"

Subodh puffed at the cigarette for one last time and opened the door. There were some four people there.

"Uncle, I am Prajesh."

"Kona, get me a candle in the verandah. Please, come in, Prajesh."

He has placed a few chairs in the verandah this noon. Kona placed a candle on the shelf. Two persons other than Prajesh came up to the verandah. Arun*babu* and Amitava. Subodh knew these people. Arun*babu* was the councilor of this ward. Amitava was his personal assistant; people of the locality, however, said that he was Arunbabu's sidekick. Subodh courteously offered them chairs. Arun*babu* wiped his sweat in the handkerchief and begun,

"I got the news while returning from the municipality. Very sad! How is boudi doing now?"

"Dr. Sen has examined her. She is feeling better now."

"Did she eat something?"

"Yes, she atea bit a few minutes back."

Subodh did not feel like talking, but continued out of courtesy.

"A boy like him! He studied in Jadavpur, isn't it?"

"Yes. History."

"That college has become their den. They are picking up meritorious boysand after brainwashing them they are taking the boys to the forests. Is this called revolution?"

Amitava's phone rang. He went ahead to receive the phone.

"Yes, tell me. We are busy now with something that has happened in our ward."

Arun made a gesture that asked him to put the phone down.

"Please call after a while!"

Arun wiped his face once again. It was really sultry today.

"Prajesh told me that CID personnel visited you."

"Yes."

"You told them everything?"

"What do you mean by everything?"

"I mean Arindam's activities, all that you are aware of."

"Arindam had been out of home for three years. During this period we had no contact with Arindam. Moreover, he also did not keep in touch with us."

"Three years!"

Arunbabu took off his spectacles and started to wipe it with the sweat soaked handkerchief itself.

"Whatever it may be, dada, I have one request to make, please co-operate with the police in all possible ways. Otherwise the harassment will only increase. Is it possible to tackle all these at your age? Moreover, you have a daughter to take care of."

"Yes, positively. I will always co-operate with the police."

"When would they hand over the body?"

"We have to go to the Shalboni Police station by 10 in the morning, the day after tomorrow."

"And after taking the body?"

"After taking the body we would come home and somewhere nearby…"

Suddenly Subodh's tongue twisted, eyes burned all of a sudden. He moved his face away from the light.

"Dada, we have a request."

Subodh raised his face.

"Do not bring the body here. I do not think the public reaction would be good. After all, everyone is angry with the Maoists. Only yesterday I saw that the Home Minister has said, "The Maoists are the gravest threat to the country's internal security.""

The bulb in the verandah came to life. Arunbabu got up.

"I must leave now. Just inform us if you need anything. Prajesh is theman of your locality."

Subodh nodded. Everyone left. Subodh sat on the stool for sometime.

"Kona, switch off the light, please."

Kona was just behind the door.

"Would you eat something, Baba?"

"No."

"Shall I serve you tea?"

"No … I do not feel like having anything now."

Subodh turned his face and tried to smile to show his daughter. Kona switched off the light. She groaned once again on her way to her mother's room; she had never seen her father weep.

3

It was difficult to look at the reddish road that goes out of the police station into the village for long in this scorching sunshine. Subodh turned his eyes away from it. His sister-in-law and her husband had arrived last morning. This one family he could call his only relation. Durjoy runs an electronic gadget shop at Shibpur. He had driven all this long way. The eldest son of Durjoy, Shantanu has brought along with him two of his friends. The younger son had stayed back in Subodh's home. "At least one male member should stay in the home," Rina had told Subodh.

"Would you like to have some tea, Subodh*da*?"

"Let's have some."

Durjoy hailed a dark complexioned boy and ordered tea.

"When would they call? Did you come to know anything?"

"Rubbish. These assholes are lazy to their bones. They would not allow us to see the body until the second-officer arrives here. He has gone to the adjacent village on routine round. And if he is blown off today, in how many years they would hand the body over, only these bastards can say!"

Durjoy failed to control himself when angry. Arindam did not like Durjoy for this. Three years ago Arindam left his administrative job (WBCS) in order to join some school, run by an NGO. He had a fierce altercation with Subodh at night. Subodh told him clearly that had he joined the NGO, he would have to leave this home. Arindam was ready. They next day even Durjoy counseled him a lot, "If you do not like the job, I'll let you become my business partner. Such a brilliant chap like you …"

Ujjala had called him, to counsel his son. "Does anyone leave a job when the market conditions are such poor?" In reply Arindam smiled a bit and left home the very next day. He must have changed a lot.

"Durjoy, will we be able to see Arindam at all?"

"What do you mean, Subodh*da*?"

"Listen, if in the meanwhile he had rotted…"

"Oh, no! They have the facility here. And why are you losing heart this way? You are crumbling for a son who was a scoundrel?"

"Baba, please listen."

Shantanu called Durjoy inside the police station.

Durjoy, who was about to pull out his packet of cigarettes, kept it back and got up to go.

"Sir, would you give me some money? I would eat."

Subodh scrutinized the boy. A naked boy of six or seven-year-old. A white line had formed above his lips. The mucus had come out of his nose and dried there. He rummaged through his pocket and handed over a ten rupee note to the boy. The moment he got the money the boy ran, straight down that road towards the village. The police station was quiet. Subodh enjoyed sitting under the tree.

"Sir, are you Subodh Bhattacharya?"

Subodh was a bit annoyed. Camera and boom once again. Even yesterday a chap came for an interview. Kona repeatedly requested him not to film them. But, the chap managed to photograph them!And the photo has come out in today's newspaper, they say.

"Please, I am not feeling well. No interview for the day."

"Sir, we are not journalists."

Subodh looked at the two young men closely. They were wearing jeans and t-shirts. The two had bags that could carry camera, at their back.

"I am Prabir and he is Prithwidev. We are documentary film makers."

But the matter was all the same; an interview. Subodh folded his hands.

"Please, let me stay alone for a while."

"Sir, we will not bother you. We would only give you an information."

Prithwidev spoke for the first time.

"Arindam*da*was not a Maoist."

Subodh's head swiveled. He clung to the cemented pedestal hard.

"We have got the proof."

Prabir lowered his bag and sat beside Subodh.

"Actually we were making a documentary on Adivasi education. We were not getting permission to shoot here. We came to know Arindam*da* then. He arranged for the shoot at his school. Reading the news the day before, we cancelled our shooting in Orissa and have come straight here. When we came and inquired in the police station they told us about you."

4

Arindam was coming out of a hut. The sky-blue colored pajama and the red panjabi that he was wearing were given to him by Ujjala during the Durga Puja. He was looking good with a head full of bushy hair complemented by a beard. The camera was following his legs from the behind. Light dust raised as his slipper struck the road on every step taken. Two kids were waiting at the turn of a road. The kids were holding a slate and some books under their arms. Arindam scratched their head and moved ahead. He took a boy on his lap from his father and asked,

"How is he doing today?"

The father nodded to say yes. The boy entered his hand inside the hair and beard of Arindam and began to play. Arindam kissed on the boy's cheek.

For the first time the camera had caught Arindam spanning the full screen of the television set. The whole twenty-one-inch of the television screen displayed the rugged face of Arindam. Kona stared at the TV without batting an eyelid.

The boys and girls sat under a tree. Arindam would give them a lesson on alphabets today.

'A', 'B'…

His voice was as enchanting as before. After showing this much the moderator went back to the discussion. Those two young men were in the studio as well. They have invited Subodh too, but he did not join them. The two men did bulk of the talking. They spoke on the making of the movie and Arindam's mission. And the two representatives of the ruling and the opposition party got entangled in a fresh broil on the development or the absence of it concerning the tribal.

The doorbell was ringing. Today Subodh has forgotten to take the thick plastic sheet in the balcony away. Arun and Amitava were standing outside the door.

"Dada, we needed to speak to you."

"Come inside."

"Did everything go well on that day?"

"Yes, everything went well."

"How are you and how is boudi now?

"We are doing fine. You wanted to say something."

"Yes, we mean our government is really ashamed for this matter concerning Arindam. The whole thing has been inadvertent. We mean… So, the Chief Minister has declared a compensation."

"I know. I saw it in the news."

Amitava's phone rung. He put the phone on silent mode without receiving it. Silence descended on the verandah. In a melodious note some soap company was advertising the quality of their product on television.

"We have another request for you."

Arun tried to break the prevailing stiffness around.

"Tell me."

"A chap like Arindam is the pride of the locality. So under the aegis of our development society we will hold a memorial meeting and a football tournament."

Subodh raised his face and looked at them; his jaw stiffened.

The moderator has gone back to the documentary from the discussion. At first there was the mutilated body of Arindam. Dried maroon colored blood was around the deep bullet wound under the throat. Ujjalashrunk her face in the pillow and groaned. Arindam's entire face was held in a close up … that right cheek where Subodh had planted a kiss after covering the bullet wound with his hand during identification...

The scene in the camera changed. That stretch of the road, which had gone to the village, while one exited the police station was shown. There three naked kids stood and watched the camera footage. Subodh sat erect. Which is the boy whom he gave the ten rupee note to? He could not recognize. He found all of them to be the same.

The camera had entered the village now. A broken verandah of a tilted house was on the frame. A few slices of sun lay stretched on it enjoying their stay there. Some houses were visible beyond the nearby bushes and shrubs. Faces of couple of women peeped. As the camera roved the faces disappeared behind the walls. An old man sat on the verandah. "How are you all here?" Someone asked. He was not seen on camera. On the whole screen two eyes, surrounded by wrinkled flesh stared without a blink. Even after waiting for long the answer did not come. The camera got up. Begin to stroll. In between there was space and beyond it plam-leaf-thatched houses. And this road had gone far, far away keeping these on its side. Did Arindam know where this road would take one to?

The road took a left turn after going some distance. A two storied concrete house was there on the turn. In red letters "Martyrs' Home" was written on the top of the house. The camera filmed the entire house in great detail. By the side of the house a couple of mud houses had sprung up in a lackluster way. A memorial column, very old, was there in front of the building. There it was indistinctly written "artyrs' column." Time had eaten up the letter M.

Based on a Fake Story

"In the rainy reason mind refuses to reason,
There is endless downpour
Amidst it I remember you."

Kanchana moved towards the seats ahead of her after singing these lines once more. There was less number of people in the compartment after the train had crossed Naihati. It was easy to pass the handful of people who stood carelessly and proceed to the seats ahead. Tua slipped through the vacant space between two seats and was spreading her arms in front of everyone. Among eight people one or two gave alms, the rest touched there forehead in a gesture of refusal. Tua passed on the loose coins to her mother once some accumulated in her small palm. Kanchana grabbed those in a fist and slipped the same in the cloth bag that hung from her left shoulder.

Nowadays Kanchana while on work looked at no one. She fixed her eyes on the wall at the end of the compartment. Initially, she had a sense of unease. Her eyes used to roam. She felt shaken in front of the glare of the gaping eyes. Her voice trembled.

Even Tua refused to sever ties with her mother's apron strings. Kanchana used to push her. She used to spread her arms recoiling within. Tua's ear lobes used to turn red in hesitation and shame. Now even she has got used to this. Tua picked up dust from the platform the moment she came to the station in the morning and rubbed it on her two cheeks. At the initial days some people used to lovingly pinch her fair cheeks and pressed a one rupee coin in her palms. Some pinched hard. Though she revolted inwardly, but in front of everyone she used to hang her head on her chest. On one night Tua lodged a mild protest to her mother in this regard as she sat beside her at the Titagarh station. Hearing her say it, the blind old woman who sat by their side had said, "Listen you gal, the next time you board a train rub some dust from the platform on your cheeks. No one will touch those again."

The train was entering Halisahar. It would be good to embark on the return journey from here. It would not be prudent to proceed any further. Kanchana with her eyes signaled Tua to come to the doors of the compartment. Tua slipped the coins that were in her palms inside her mother's cloth bag. Kanchana after getting down from the train went to the other side of the platform to catch a down train and sat for a while in a corner. Tua took a few steps to roam around the station and later on sat beside her mother with knees folded and coaxed, "Will you buy me a cake, ma?" Kanchana unmindfully nodded, the gesture signifying that even today Tua's coaxing would not bear fruit.

"Dada, what is the time?" Kanchana asked. One aged man after removing the bidi from his lips answered, "It could be 1.30 pm." As per Kanchana's calculation there were still twenty minutes to go before the down train would arrive and if the calculation failed it could be close to an hour. Tua in the meanwhile had got up and was roaming in the platform. "Hey Tua, come here." Kanchana hailed her daughter, but Tua failed to ignore her mother's call. The moment she arrived Kanchana grabbed her hair and forced her to sit by her side. "If you do not loaf around you don't feel satisfied, isn't it? Had the train come now you would have stayed here all alone," she told her daughter. Actually that was not the case; she failed to tell her daughter the real reason behind her flaring up. Even a year ago their address was Ranaghat, a forty-minute train ride from here. From the very first day Prasanta had asked her not to venture into this route. But in spite of that she at times does come on this route. Because the way she had got accustomed to this route, she wasn't with the others. Last week she mistakenly boarded a train at Dankuni that took her to an unknown station called Belmuri. The next train to get back to Dankuni was at 8 pm. It was then only 6.30 in the evening. She had been mentally calculating whether she would get a train to return to Dum Dum from Dankuni. Suddenly someone placed a hand on her bun of hair. It was not just placing of a hand, an unknown woman had taken control of the bun. "You rascal bitch, why have you come on this route? Does your father stay here?" Observing what had been unfolding, a couple of hawkers wanted to know, "What is the matter, Mukto masi?"

"What else? The bitch entered my compartment at Dankuni. From there, this far... the slut has eaten into my entire business," the woman thundered.

Tua had then just bit into one biscuit from the remaining four that was left in the packet of Parle G that was bought at noon. When she heard the word, "Oh God!" in her mother's voice she turned only to see that a dark complexioned woman was dragging her mother by the hair. The woman was plumb, she wore a sari as ladies would when at home; her eyes were so wrinkled that at one glance she would appear to be a blind woman. Tua immediately ran and grabbed her mother. The woman paid no regard to the fact that she stomped on Tua's little hands in her jest to drag Kanchana down as fast as she could. She dragged Kanchana to the furthest end of the platform, made her slump to the ground and thundered,

"Tell me you wicked bitch, why you ventured into this route? Show me your card."

Kanchana in the meanwhile touched her disheveled hair and had begun to sob.

I came on this route by mistake. I did not realize. Masi, pardon me this time," Kanchana implored.

Bochon*da* on behalf of the Dum Dum Hawkers' Union had written Kanchana a letter and had warned,

"Do not show this to anyone apart from the railway police and TT. You can go anywhere in the main line from Barrackpore to Naihati, from Durganagar to Barasat but do not venture beyond Baranagar on the Dankuni line. That area is under a different union. If any trouble occurs we would be in no position to do anything. And come and attend our marches and protests, do not disappear with this. Every week you will give him … Bhisnu, come here."

Hearing the call a bearded man of short stature came limping.

"You will hand him over the weekly membership fee," Bochon*da* said.

"Every Friday, at 7 pm. Listen masi, you will not default. Lots of problems arise later. I do not like trouble…"

Bochon silenced Bhisnu.

"The money is required for you people only later on. You know we have to organize protest, demonstration if attempts are made to evict you all or there is police harassment on people like you? Those things do not happen without spending money! What do you say? Let it be. Remember what I have told you. Do not give this letter to anyone," Bochon urged.

Therefore, from the first day itself Kanchana did not show the letter to anyone. She will not show it to the woman too, she had decided beforehand. But the woman was not easy to escape from. Kanchana had ventured on to a new route and had dipped her hands in her earnings, so she was not ready to allow the matter to settle down that easily. He had heard that caught in such a trouble at the Habra station one had lost the entire earnings. Remembering this Kanchana with both hands had grabbed her bag. On the other hand Mukto masi was determined to see her card. The dogged lady now went for Kanchana's bag. As a result, Tua too jumped on the bag. Failing to take hold of the bag Mukto masi attacked Kanchana. She went on slapping Kanchana. Some slaps landed on Tua. At last, amidst mediation of other hawkers both Kanchana and Tua were brought to the hawkers' union office just outside the platform. The secretary of the union was then present in the bamboo made room that had roof made of earthen tiles. The secretary was a man of medium built with earthen colored complexion. On his lips was the residual portion of a burning bidi that was not puffed at for long. He was reading a piece of paper with all attention. Hearing the sound of many entering his office, he folded the piece of paper, kept it on the cheap table and in a disgusted tone asked,

"What is the matter?"

Mukto masi came forward and started to retell the tale. By the time Mukto masi had told half her tale, the secretary was horribly annoyed. He addressed someone called Gulle.

"Gulle, do I not have any other work to do? All rubbish. What do you all do sitting in this room. No one henceforth should enter office with such trifles."

Hearing what the secretary had to say Gulle brought Mukto masi, Kanchana and all others who had accompanied them outside the office and attentively listened to what had happened. After listening to everybody he wanted to see the letter that Kanchana carried. This time Kanchana did not refuse to show. After seeing the letter Gulle passed his judgment; Kanchana had to pay Mukto masi a fine of rupees fifty. Kanchana begged and turned it to twenty. When after taking twenty bucks Mukto masi left hurling abuses at Kanchana it was nine at night. They reached Dankuni at 11.30 pm. There was no hope of returning to Dum Dum. Even if they returned they would no way be able to go to Durganagar tonight. Tua did not have the strength to walk any further. She was hungry. Above all, she was feeling sleepy. That was for the first time that Kanchana spent a whole night at a station.

She was not expecting any such trouble in this route. Kanchana knew everybody well who worked on this route. But the trouble on the other route was very different. When Prasanta came to know of what had happened for the first time he had said,

"Wasn't there any other route barring this?"

Kanchana did not reply. Nowadays she on most of the occasions did not reply to Prasanta's comments. Had it been earlier she should have said something. Prasanta left the letter open on the floor and stood up.

"What is the matter? Did you not hear what I said?"

Kanchana did not reply to this as well; instead she picked up the letter from the floor and said in an angry tone,

"Do not forget that this letter is the only avenue that you have to keep yourself fed twice daily."

Prasanta pretended not to have heard this and asked, "Is there some kind of lure in this route?"

"Yes, there is," Kanchana replied.

Prasanta's whole body stiffened in anger. But there was nothing that could be done. So he sat again on the mat spread on the floor. They did not have any bed here. In this one room in the slum of Italgacha all that they had to call their own were a mat, some clothes for the three of them, one pan that was transformed into a cooker when they cooked rice and two plates. One plate belonged to Prasanta. Kanchana and Tua ate out of the same plate.

"You know, your going on that route may not be good for us. If someone spots you!" Prasanta said.

 Prasanta told this calmly.

"What could be done? I do not know the other routes. How can I go in those routes?" Kanchana replied as she was pouring just bought uncooked rice on the plate. Prasanta only sighed in response and said,

"Do not go towards Ranaghat ever."

A down train was coming. Kanchana picked up her bag. Tua too got up. Some people began to run after entering the platform to get into the compartments that were ahead of them. Kanchana would on purpose get into one of the last compartments. She would change compartments and proceed after the train would leave Naihati. It happened to be the ladies' compartment that became stationary where Kanchana stood on the platform. Kanchana made Tua embark first then she got into the train after Tua. Tua immediately went inside on the left hand side. She knew her mother would begin her job soon. The train began to move. The moment it left the platform Kanchana began,

> *"You filled my soul, you quenched my thirst,*
> *Give me more of life, O' Lord!"*

Some women who were seated looked at them with annoyance. Kanchana had begun the song on a scale higher than the normal. Otherwise in this droning noise of the train her thin melodious voice wouldn't reach anyone. Like girls of her age she too started to take lessons in music in her childhood. She had a good voice. That was why his father enrolled her in a music school. Kanchana's father ran a small grocery shop at Joynagar. Now her elder brother looks after the same. Kanchana had good relation with him as well until last year since her marriage. Now that is not the case. As a result, she could not go there even after leaving home. Because there too Prasanta was most wanted.

She failed to do good business in this compartment today. Only six rupees. They got down the moment they arrived at Kankinada. They had to move fast towards the next compartment the moment they got down. There was this problem whenever they boarded the ladies' compartment. The next compartment was that of the vendors'. It became difficult to move ahead amidst the hullabaloo of loading and unloading goods. The train was about to leave the moment they reached the general compartment ahead of the vendors'. Someone dragged Tua inside the compartment. And Kanchana almost jumped into the compartment. The crowd in this compartment was much more than that in the ladies compartment. However, that was not a problem. She could do good business in such compartments as these.

She will commence her work after finding her way into the compartment. Many had crowded the area in front of the doors. "Dada, please give us space; we want to go inside," said Kanchana. Kanchana tried to make it to the inside of the compartment as she said this. Some gave them the space to move.

Some looked at them with annoyance in their eyes. She carefully skirted such glances. She mentally decided to begin with a song devoted to the Mother, Goddess Kali, in this compartment. The song, *"Mother, you and your many hues…"* came to her lips. The day her mother-in-law came to see her for the first time, her elder brother wanted her to sing this song. Her mother-in-law had liked it. The next day after the bride-rice ceremony of the marriage ritual she had invited the whole locality for a musical afternoon in the post lunch time. After coming to know that it will be devotional songs devoted to Kali, Bindu masi of the locality said,

"Oh good child, do you not know kirtan? If you know sing one."

Kanchana did not know how to sing kirtans, so she said,

"I do not know how to sing kirtan that much."

She was ashamed to say this, she covered her face with the hood she had on her head using the sari that she wore. Bindu masi had a reputation in the locality for calling a spade a spade.

"How is this, O' new bride! You have learnt so much music, but haven't learnt how to sing a kirtan? Anyway, sister, from now on you will have the good fortune to listen to modern songs!" Bindu masi said.

As she made gestures to leave the place after saying this to Kanchana's mother-in-law, she became a bit embarrassed.

"Why don't you sit for a while, didi? Kanchana, you told me that you know Baul songs. Why don't you sing one?" Kanchana's mother-in-law said.

Kanchana nodded in reply. Though Bindu masi sat on request from couple of more people, but she was unhappy. Kanchana sang. Everyone acknowledged,

"No didi, you have been lucky to get a daughter-in-law like this. What a melodious voice she has got!"

The only thing Bindu masi said was, "Yes." After being egged on by some people she added, "Wish she could sing kirtan…" Sampa masi stopped her and said, "Since she is here during the winter she would learn kirtan too, such hullabaloo you make over kirtans at that time." She smiled a smile, and then told a few lighter things that one could anticipate to be in store for the new bride. Kanchana after that did not get the opportunity to sing in accompaniment of a harmonium. Such things were not entertained in an in-law's place is a mufassil town. At times she would play the Dhoom channel in television in a low key and in a key lower than that would hum the tunes of modern Bengali songs. Her audience was she alone and at the dead of the night Prasanta. He would rub his just shaven face on Kanchana's soft cheeks and would coax,

"Why don't you sing a song?"

"Which one?" she used to ask in a loving tone.

"Oh that song in the "Premer Kahini" (Love Story) … 'Here goes the love story…'" Prasanta himself sung to give her the cue. Kanchana would sing the song from where Prasanta left in a hushed tone. Prasanta's love probed deeper.

Tua dropped some coins inside Kanchana's bag and proceeded towards the next seats. Kanchana repeated the two lines in the prelude for couple of times. She failed to remember the next lines. She had this problem on the first day itself. She felt like crying once she got down from the train that day. But, in the next three months she had realized that she could get money in train even by singing an entire song in the wrong way but she would have to passionately display her poverty. As a result she jumped couple of lines and was now on a new line. The train had almost reached Palta. Here she would have to change the compartment once again. She stopped the line in between and poured her poverty in the compartment full of passengers—

"Dada, my husband has no work to go to. He has been confined indoors following an accident. I have a little daughter. Please donate as much as you can, keeping the little girl in mind," she said.

She winded up what she had to say fast. Neither was there time nor need for anything more. She has had a good collection in this compartment. Tua had thrice entered her hands into her bag. "Dada, will you get down?" she asked as she tried to find her way out of the compartment holding Tua's hand.

Train has touched the platform. She first helped Tua to get down. She hurried towards the next compartment the moment she got down. There was a sizeable crowd as there had been no trains for some time now. Even before she could reach the doors of the next compartment she felt that someone had placed a hand on her shoulders.

"You are Tulu's wife? Aren't you?" A man asked.

"Hey guys, Tulu's wife has arrived." That was for the first time Kanchana heard that name. They had just got down from the car. The mother and sister-in-law were yet to perform the customary puja before receiving the new bride inside the house. From that moment onwards she had just become Tulu's wife. She only checked her name as Kanchana while tallying her name in the voter slip. Even Prasanta would have forgotten her official name had not the checks he received as commission come in her name. During the 2010-11 the name Tulu had become synonymous with dream in the whole of Ranaghat. At least seven young men of his locality were immersed in the dream of taking home fat commission checks after they spent their whole day with Tulu planning to make dreams reach the common household. Prasanta had in the meanwhile after leaving his rupees eight thousand-a-month job with a private organization become 'Tulu', engrossed in raising different kinds of funds for the chit fund firm Sharada. Beginning from the tea vendors, the rickshaw pullers to the moneyed men of the locality, all were riding Tulu's dream. By eight in the morning

Prasanta used to hold meetings with all the agents below his rank in the drawing room. Kanchana also got up in the morning and left a flask full of tea in that room. Prasanta had got some cups made of plastic. Then around 10 or 10.30 am he, after taking an early lunch, went out for client meetings. He bought a motorbike during the Durga Puja of 2011.

"It is not possible to roam about in a cycle the whole day, let's buy a motorbike. What do you say?" Prasanta had asked Kanchana.

Prasanta broached the topic as he observed the check worth rupees thirty-two thousand that had arrived on that day.

"It would be worth it. You can drop Tua at school. I will then discontinue with the school van. At times the van driver does not come and is always on the lookout of increasing the fees," Kanchana had said.

After about a week the vehicle bought on installment reached home. The next day Tua pulled everyone out of bed at five in the morning.

"Baba, get up. Won't you drop me at school?" Tua said.

Prasanta watched the clock with sleepy eyes.

"Your school starts at 10.30 am. What will you do now?" Prasanta inquired.

"Get up. Brush your teeth or else we will be late," Tua had implored.

Irritated Kanchana beat her daughter up a bit for such an unjust hurry.

"On other days you cry when asked to go to school; but today! Go back to sleep, I say," Kanchana scolded Tua.

That day Tua's granny called everyone and told and retold this story. On the other hand Prasanta's platoon of seven had become thirty-five. Among them there were around eight women.

"Can the ladies do all such things," bewildered Kanchana had asked.

"The success ratio of girls is higher than that of the boys. You do not know how they can coax!" Prasanta had said with a smile and added, "Don't you understand from your own example; how you convince me and buy a new sari every month."

"Oh ho, is buying a new sari same as forking out money from others?" asked Kanchana.

"It's all the same," Prasanta said.

"Then even I can do it?" asked Kanchana.

"If you try you could," assured Prasanta.

Prasanta became sleepy.

"Then employ me!" Kanchana coaxed.

"Our daughter is growing up. We will have to get her married. The market prices are soaring… what will happen after twenty years? What, have you fallen asleep?" Kanchana tried to reason.

Kanchana pushed Prasanta to find out whether he had really fallen asleep. Prasanta made an interjection, "Hmmm," to prove that he was listening.

"What, have you fallen asleep?" Kanchana asked again.

"No," was Prasanta's curt reply. Kanchana placed her chin on Prasanta's chest and started to draw patterns of solace there with her fingers.

"Why don't you take me? Please!" Kanchana implored.

"I will consider and let you know tomorrow," replied Prasanta.

"Why tomorrow? Tell me today. It will ease things even for you," Kanchana reasoned.

"Who will look after our daughter?" Prasanta was practical.

"How do the other girls manage?" Kanchana retorted.

"My mother might object. Even my elder brothers…" Prasanta was at a loss.

Kanchana did not prolong the conversation. Prasanta had given an infallible logic. Kanchana within a week of her marriage had realized that though the elder bothers led their own families their way living in the same house, yet they had an invisible switch in their hands to control matters concerning home and family. After coming back from her mother's place that she visited for the first time after marriage as part of the whole ritual, her husband had made a plan for a honeymoon trip to Darjeeling. When he told this to his elder brothers, the middle one said, "Then go. But Darjeeling is a bit costly. Why don't you try Digha instead?"

Kanchana had been to Digha five times before marriage. She had started to dislike the same old sea, the same crowd and the accompanying nuisance. She had never been to Darjeeling. After the ritual of coming back from her mother's place she silently had packed her bag with some light clothes and had landed in the very known sea beach of Digha. The elder brothers did not go anywhere. Then her daughter was born. She failed to realize how 2011 passed and there came 2012. Prasanta slowly got immersed in work then got drowned in it.

Now they had little time to talk. He got irritated as she tried to broach a conversation. He had no fixed time to bathe and eat. Different kinds of people come to him. Kanchana knew none of them. In the month of March one person rode to their home in a motorbike, gave Prasanta a letter. At night Kanchana asked, "What was that letter about, would you tell?" Prasanta did not reply. The next morning the eldest among his brothers called him and asked, "Did you not pay the installments of your motorbike?"

"Why?" asked Prasanta.

"Yesterday a man had come to Madhu's shop. He was looking for you. I gave the address. When he was returning I asked, "Did you meet him," he said, "No." Then I came to know. He told if you failed to clear the dues by this month he would confiscate the bike. What is the matter?" his eldest brother asked.

Prasanta sipped his tea in silence. The eldest brother again wanted to know "Why don't you speak?" Prasanta took another sip of the tea and said,

"Some payment has got stuck since January. Some maturity payment has also got stuck. Big sum of money. The client needed it badly. I gave the client money from my account to settle the issue. As a result I could not deposit my installment amount. All the checks would get realized by this month, the Kolkata office of my firm has informed. The moment I will get those I will clear everything…," Prasanta said in one breath.

The payment, however, could not be given. On April 12 they confiscated the vehicle from the road itself. Tua could not go to school until April 14. She would not go to school by any other means than her father's motorbike. No one knew where Prasanta was for the whole day on April 15. Almost on every minute a person had visited his home looking for him. At one point in time the wife of his middle brother said, "Why on earth would we put up with all these trouble? It's all yours so you take care." That day

Kanchana realized that she was as if standing in the middle of a big open ground. She did not know which direction to go to from here!

Prasanta came back at midnight. When asked he said,

"I went to Kolkata."

"Throughout the day many people came looking for you. What has happened? In the TV…" Kanchana could not complete the sentence.

"The company has folded. Neither the CEO, nor the CMD could be traced… no one," Prasanta blurted out and sat on the bed without changing his clothes. Kanchana had never seen him so devastated.

"Now what will I do? From where will I get such huge sum of money? People will kill me!" Prasanta said.

Kanchana pressed the unkempt head against her breasts and said to give him solace,

"Do not worry, God will set everything right. You did not waste the money yourself. The company did. If the company has downed shutters why should you pay?"

They could not sleep the rest of the night. Early in the morning Kanchana's phone rang. "Dada! So early in the morning?" People were visiting even the place where Kanchana's elder brother lived. Prasanta's phone had been kept switched off, so…

From early in the morning in the office room outside there were so many people that space became insufficient. Everyone wanted to know, "What will happen? Will we get our money back?" Prasanta gave them assurance. "Dada, company will undoubtedly return all your money. Just wait for a few days." Some had faith in what he said some didn't believe. Prasanta now used the most vital weapon in his arsenal. "Dada even if the company isn't there, I am here. Let the company not give, but I will give. Just wait for a few days."

A week passed in waiting. Some investors in the meanwhile had gone to Kolkata they spewed fire after returning in terms with reality there. The news telecast in the TV fanned the fire. Prasanta got angry, "You all are listening to hearsay. I am telling you everything would be fine. I am here. Do not listen to wild rumors. Everybody is conspiring," Prasanta said. The public anger only increased.

"Bastard, everybody is telling a lie, only you and Sudipta Sen are the truth-saying Yudhishthira. Isn't it? I am giving you two days. If I do not get the money…," warned one of the investors.

Prasanta spent the whole day calculating. In all, rupees forty lakh will have to be returned. But putting together all he had, the savings and the jewelries of Kanchana, it would not be more than two lakh rupees. "What will I do now? Now I have no option but to commit…" Kanchana groaned hearing Prasanta say this. She had heard in the evening news bulletin that two agents at South 24 Parganas had hung themselves to death.

If we tell your elder brothers won't they give you the money worth your share in this house? Kanchana asked. "I told borda (the eldest brother). He said as long as our mother was alive the house will not be divided," Prasanta said.

In the next morning Prasanta went out with his bank pass book and Kanchana's jewelries and returned in the evening. Until late at night he was meeting people one by one and after lot of cajoling them was convincing each to accept some money. Trouble began when the payment procedure was drawing to a close. A person's daughter was to get married. He had deposited the entire sum of two lakh rupees that he got as PF at the end of his service tenure. He needs the entire money back. He was unwilling to take twenty thousand rupees. First he left in a very angry mood only to return with his men. First they shouted, then they threatened then they started beating up Prasanta. Within 12.30 at night the whole drawing room of Prasanta's looked like a scrap dealers' storage room. Prasanta's whole face had bruises. Blood had dried after coming out of the corner of his mouth. The pocket of his shirt got torn and was hanging. Kanchana had herself bought the shirt during the last Durga Puja from Big Bazaar of Kolkata.

"Where are you going to so early in the morning?"

Kanchana asked as she spotted Prasanta put on his shirt. Outside it was still dark.

"I will go to the Kolkata office," Prasanta replied.

"Go when the light comes out," said an anxious Kanchana.

"No it would be late," Prasanta said.

Prasanta almost ran out of the house. Kanchana ran after him some distance and asked,

"When will you return?"

"It will be night," Prasanta replied.

The night came and went. One, two, three nights. Prasanta did not return. People came to the home searching for him throughout the days. There ensued shouting, abuses and threats. Tua had not been able to go to school. Kanchana had spent terror-stricken nights on bed after switching off the lights of the room. Every time she thought that someone must be banging at the door outside, that someone will kick open the door at once.

Someone tapped on the window twice. What was the time at night then? It was difficult to guess in the darkness. Kanchana raised her ears to listen. Was it an illusion? Again it happened. Thrice, someone tapped on the window. Kanchana thought whether she should reply or not; again the noise happened. This time it was louder and continued for a bit more duration. Kanchana went to the window and asked in a hushed voice, "Who is it?" After a few seconds the reply came, "Open the door! I am Tulu."

Kanchana shuddered after hearing the name after a span of six months. She turned and saw it was an old man. The man questioned again, "Aren't you Tulu's wife?" Kanchana did not reply. She grabbed Tua's hand and moved ahead fast. The train would leave. She would have to get into a compartment. The man did not give up the trail. He was almost running after them. Kanchana dashed a couple of people in a bid to move ahead. Somehow she managed to get into a compartment. The train had begun to move. The man jumped into the moving train. The people standing at the gate gave an anxious cry. "Grandpa you would have been sucked into the wheels by now," one of the passengers said. The man paid scant regard to such comments. He pushed his way through the crowd and came inside the compartment and after standing behind Kanchana, gasped, "You are Tulu's wife. Aren't you?" Irritated Kanchana queried, "What do you want? Who are you?" Tua clung to her mother's apron string. Some people in the compartment had observed the proceedings. Some cast their glaring glance at the old man. The old man closely scrutinized Kanchana. "No I did not make any mistake. You are Kanchana. This is your daughter, isn't it? What was your name? ... Anjali. Isn't it?" When he attempted to touch Tua's chin Kanchana pushed the hand away. Then a young man standing on the side placed his hand on the shoulder of the old man. "What is happening, dadu? What is the problem?"

"Nothing, son. These people are my acquaintances," the old man replied.

"No, dada, I do not know this old man at all," Kanchana protested in a shout.

"Don't say like that, you do not know me? I am Kesto Majhi. After your marriage once Tulu and you came to my house. You had ripe mangoes. Don't you remember? You may not remember, but Tulu does," the old man said.

"Dadu, you go to Tulu then. Do you want to go to jail in a rape case at this old age?" the young man said.

The old man smiled a bit.

"Yes son, people who ought to be in jail enjoy life these days. And we… The person the mango of whose tree they ate, even ate the two lakh rupees of the PF and turned me into a beggar… they even fail to recognize me. So I will have to go to jail…"

The look in the eyes of the people in the compartment changed a bit. The old man got emboldened by this.

"You do not believe in what I am saying? Go and ask the others who are there in the compartment behind this," the old man said. "We are all going to the commission's office today to deposit our papers. Just wait, I will make a telephone call…," as the old man said this he fished out a mobile from his pocket, searched the number out and began to dial.

"Paltu, come to the number four compartment from the beginning of the train. Come fast. I have got her! I told you all the lass was Tulu's wife. Come soon. Yes. Get down at Barrackpore and get into this compartment. What did you say? I could not get you properly. Just get down."

In the fast pace of the event those who were in favor of Kanchana a minute before had a change of heart. They now pretended that nothing had transpired here till now. Kanchana had shrunk in an unknown fear. Generally the train before entering Barrackpore from Palta halts at least once. She thought that she would jump off the compartment the moment the train stopped. What would happen would happen. But Tua? It would be fraught with risk if Tua had to be made to jump as well. But the train did not stop today. Though it slowed down a bit but it entered Barrackpore in a stretch. The old man proceeded to the doors of the compartment the moment the train stopped. However, he kept an eye on Kanchana. On the other hand one or two people being influenced by the high pitched rendering of the story of the old man being cheated had by now encircled Kanchana so that she doesn't manage to flee. He addressed them,

"Just see, dada, that she does not manage to escape. … Paltu, this way please… come, board the compartment."

Kanchana's heart jumped. The day Kanchan's drawing room was ransacked this man had also been there.

"Is this the bitch?" the man asked.

The man started to roll up the sleeves of his shirt as he proceeded.

"Where is Tulu?" he asked Kanchana.

"I do not know anyone. I am telling you the truth," Kanchana said.

Kanchana knew that at this moment the only thing that could save her was her tears.

"You do not know! Two smacks will make you know everything you bitch. You thought you would run away and get saved. Tell me, where is that bastard?"

Kanchana folded her hands and began to sob—

"I am telling you, dada, I do not know. Had he been there would I have to join the line to work! One night he came, lured us out of home, brought us to the Howrah station, made us seat in the station and disappeared, never to return again. I am telling the truth, dada! I swear on my daughter," Kanchana begged.

The old man then came forward through the crowd.

"At first she failed to recognize me. Now she is remembering everything. Force the woman out of this compartment and into this station. It must have to be a combined effort of all to get information out of her," the old man said.

The train had just touched the Titagarh station. The man forced Kanchana out of the compartment. Tua failed to keep pace with that force; she stumbled. Kanchana tried to steady her, but failed. The man with a fierce tug thrust her on the platform. Tua embraced her mother. Her eyes watered too out of fear. "Ouch!" The man had stomped on Kanchana's right leg with his left leg.

It was deep into the night then. The platform number four put on a deserted look. The old blind lady had bought tea worth three rupees in a glass. "Come, pour the tea and drink it. Did you get to eat anything throughout the day? Even the kid I think…" The old lady put the glass down on the concrete of the platform. It has been an hour now that Kanchana and Tua had come out of the office of the railway police. The old lady was sitting outside the office. God knows how the information reached her! Tua spotted her first. "Mother, the blind dida!" Kanchana had not noticed at all. The GRP constable in the round at Titagarh platform rescued Kanchana and Tua when around 10 investors after forcing the mother and daughter into the platform had interrogated them following threats and coercion to bring out information for about 10 hours. After all their initiatives failed they were just getting physical and had begun to showers slaps and kicks on Kanchana. The investors also followed the GRP personnel and the mother-daughter duo. The constable straight way sent the mother and daughter in the room of the officer in charge. The officer after listening everything told the investors, "Okay, we will send them to the police station. You people leave. Whatever information you need to take, take from there. Now leave this place." He made everyone leave and shut the door of his office from outside.

After about twenty minutes the officer opened the doors and asked, "Where is he?" Kanchana in a gesture with which she had got accustomed in the last one-and-a-half hour said, "I am telling you the truth officer. I do not know. Had I known would I have begged on the streets?" The officer scrutinized her for a minute or so and said, "Alright, stay here until night falls, and then leave this place."

What was the time of the night could not be said as there was no watch in this room. Kanchana repeatedly scrutinized the only blouse that she has got. Without a stitch it could not be worn any more. She had made Tua count the money. No money has been lost. Twenty-six rupees. She will have to arrange for a needle at night. She took a sip from the tea and asked the old woman, "Do you have a needle?"

"Why?"

"The blouse has got absolutely torn. It cannot be worn anymore. Please give. I will give it back to you tomorrow if I come to this side." Kanchana said.

The old lady put her hand inside her bag and brought out a needle along with half a reel of thread.

"Do not come to this line for some days now. Work on the Barasat route. Go home today daughter, do not delay any more."

Kanchana got up as she put the needle inside her bag. The down train was entering platform four.

"I take leave of you. Let's see if we could work for some fifteen rupees in this train. I will have to give the remaining thirty-five rupees that I owe the grocer today," Kanchana said as she walked to catch the down train.

Wear to Become a King

"Oh! The slipper had tobe torn now?" Samaresh is already late today. The Shantipur local of 9.02 am has come exactly forty-five minutes after the scheduled time. As a result he had to let go two trains. Finally, he had to cling to the doors of the Barrackpore local at around quarter to 10 and reached the Sealdah station at around 11 am. There isn't any scheduled arrival time in office, however, if someone fails to enter it before the new boss, Tapas Choudhuri,arrives, one would get hell from the superior, and this has been the latest trend in the office. The senior Choudhuri would somehow budge had you explained the situation to him properly, but Tapas Sir is impossible! In such a situation, the one-fifty rupees worth sandal tore after colliding with a stone that raised its head like a *Shivalinga* on the footpath at the junction of the Gray Street. While running a family within rupees seven-thousand and five-hundred, Samaresh had always tried to buy a pair of shoes that would stand him in good stead in all the seasons – summer, rain and winter. His only problem surfaced when he got invited to ceremonies. Then a mug of water, some detergent and a piece of cloth were all that he could fall back on. He had to make the old slipper look like a new one after thorough cleaning and washing. And every time he did this an annoyed Runu would say, "Buy yourself a pair of new shoes when you get your next salary. I feel ashamed to move with you in the society." Until now Samaresh has come to know that many people are ashamed to do many things with him. As a result, Runu's words fail to spur him into action. "In this world there are some men who spend their lives pretending to be unashamed." Runu grudges late at night in bed. Samaresh, with his mouth gaping, tries to get some sleep beside his daughter.

The little finger of his left leg is aching now as he dragged his feet for nearly half-a-kilometer in the drizzle before he could reach his office building. Some days ago an auto rickshaw had overrun this very finger.

"Dada, even today it seems you are late!"

He wearily smiled at the comment of the liftman while folding his umbrella. On any other day he would have scaled up the stairs to the sixth floor. He had seen in the television that the heart stayed fit that way.

You get a shiver when you enter an AC zone wearing a shirt that has got drenched in rain. Baksi*babu* was immersed in the big VAT register of the company again after lifting his eyes once as he turned his head to look at Samaresh through underneath his spectacles after he had heard the glass door of the office screech.

"Baksi*da*, where is the attendance register?"

Samaresh, finding the register not in place, asked this question to the head accountant RanenBaksi.

"You cannot sign today."

Baksi replied without looking at Samaresh.

"Why, dada? Today the train pissed me off… otherwise every day I come on time."

Samaresh tried to convince Baksi. Baksi*da* lifted his finger to point at the wall behind.

"Didn't you see the notice that was put up yesterday?"

Last evening when Choudhuri*saheb* stuck the six-line notice, printed on the office letter head, on the sky-blue wall, just opposite his desk it was supposedly quite late for Shibu, who stays as far as Mecheda. People, who as Shibu did, stayed at faraway places, were loitering around seeking opportunity to sneak out of office. One of those people Ashim*da*of Duttapukur came up to him and declared, " Samaresh, I am afraid we would not be able to work in this organization for long."

"Why, comrade? What has happened? Didn't boss release you even today? You have missed out on your 6.22 pm local train." Samaresh looked at the watch hung above Baksi*da*'s head before pulling his leg.

"Forget your 6.22! Just go and see what notice your 'voss' has put up on that wall."

"What happened again?"

"Why don't you go and see it for yourself? You will have to fucking come to office on time, but when you would get released from this pig's den is uncertain."

Ashim*da*grudgingly went back to his desk and packed his office bag. Samaresh approached the notice. The summary of what was written in the notice was that your three day pay would get deducted if you were late on three days in a month. Net seven fifty grands would simply vanish from your salary. Moreover, without special permission you could not leave the office before 7.30 pm. Samaresh gave a smile. Apart from a Sunday, he has not seen the way to his home at 7.30 pm for almost six years now!

"Yes, I have seen the notice; but can nothing be done now? Why don't you inquire, you will find that the train ran really late today!"

"Company has not appointed me to sniff around you. I will not be able to give you the register. Go and get the permission from our boss. I can give you the register only then."

On Chowdhuri*saheb*'s glass door a plastic-like material was stuck; as a result, you could not see what's inside. Standing in front of his chamber, thinking whether to enter or not Samaresh knocked on the door.

"May I come in, Sir?"

"Please."

"Sir."

"Tell me, what it is. Oh, it's you. Where had you been all this while? I called for you twice but you were not there."

"No Sir, I mean, the train was…"

"Was late, isn't it?"

"Yes, Sir."

"Okay, I am going to release you from today. If possible you join the management of the Railways from the afternoon itself. Join back office from the day trains wouldn't be running late anymore. Bloody liar."

"No Sir, I am telling you the truth."

"Shut up, you were late on six days this month. You spent the whole day to bring a payment from Bhowanipore. You think that I know nothing that's happening in the office?"

"Sir, it takes time to go to Bhowanipore and come back."

"How do you go to Bhowanipore?"

"By bus, Sir."

"How did you go there last Thursday?"

Samaresh paused. He could not decide whether to speak the truth or not. When he goes for collection it has become his practice to save on the bus fare. Not much could be saved though! But it accounts for the afternoon or the evening snack. And if he fails to find time to eat, he buys Lemons or Guavas for his daughter or a packet of *nimki* for Runu.

"I went by bus, Sir."

"Then how did you have tea at the Exide crossing? Did the tyre of the bus leak? Or the tired bus driver took time off after making you disembark at Exide?"

"No, Sir. Actually on that day due to some meeting at Bhowanipore the bus…"

"Mr. Roy, just shut up. You are not ashamed to tell lies! What would you teach your daughter? You would be marked absent today. Leave. Come on time from tomorrow, otherwise this month is going to be your last here."

Samaresh said nothing. Ashim*da* was right yesterday. It would not be possible to maintain the monthly supply of domestic ration from here for long.

"Listen!"

Mr. Choudhuri called back.

"Go to the Debdaru Estate once today. There is some problem there. Work has stopped since morning. Go there and bring me the report. Do not make good your escape as you have not signed the register."

"Dada, tea!"

Samaresh looked up from the drawer and then again went about searching it. He could recall having kept a safety pin there. He found it under the table some weeks ago. As his drawer has no lock most of the people with or without reason look through it. If someone can lay his hands on such a useful stuff likea safety pin, one will not desist from taking it. But, he couldn't get anything when he needed. Without repairing the slipper it would be impossible for him to walk today.

In this office only Ratan could give you things – from a needle to sew with to safety pins of varying sizes. Ratan sits at the entrance of the office beyond Baksi*da*'s table. Samaresh addresses Ratan as "dada." Though they were of the same age this was the only place in the office from where he would receivehonest counseling.

"Baksi*da*, I will have to go to Kasba, would you prepare a TA (Traveling Allowance) slip for me?" Samaresh addressed Baksi*da* on his way to Ratan's table.

"From now on show me the bus tickets and collect the money. This is boss' order."

On hearing this Samaresh halted on his way.

"What do you mean? Boss himself has asked me to go to Kasba."

"Then go and get the slip signed by him."

"What a problem! The money that he has in his pocket … what he would eat if he has to mend the slipper! Moreover, Kasba is faraway…"

"Dada, I was not aware of this new rule. As a result, I did not bring enough money. Tomorrow onwards…"

"This is not a new rule. It applies only on you. No one has been caught red handed as you have been yet! The day others would get caught, this rule would apply on them too."

"Look, if you do not have money, borrow from someone. You have no dearth of pals here."

Samaresh spoke no more. Dialogue begets dialogue.

Ratan*da* was seated at his desk checking some bills.

"Can you lend me a safety pin, Ratan*da*?"

"Why? What happened?"

"Just see how the slipper tore in front of Jadav's tea stall."

Ratan pushed the bills aside and took a good close look.

"It's condition is such that a safety pin would be of no help. Replace it."

"How can I replace it now? If I were to buy even a plastic sandal of a reputed brand it would cost me two-hundred bucks. I cannot afford it this month."

"Why? These days I find the Chinese sandals selling on the streets at twenty / twenty-five rupees a pair!"

"Howawful those sandals look! Moreover, if I get a skin allergy… and from today I would get the TA bills reimbursed only after I show the bus tickets. I have only fifteen rupees in my pocket. Now if I were to mend this sandal it would cost minimum ten rupees. I don't know how I will go to Kasba and come back in five rupees."

"Yes, I have heard Baksi*da* telling you this. Do one thing, I am giving you three-hundred bucks, buy a new pair of sandals. You have to walk a lot! Use what would be left after buying the sandal for travel. Go, find your way out of office; the weather is poor today. Listen, don't try and walk the distance. For some days…"

Ratan took out three-hundred bucks from his purse as he was talking. Samaresh hesitated a bit. Though he had on some earlier occasions taken money from Ratan, today he recoiled inwardly. He was never so insulted before.

"No, dada, I didn't ask for money. I do not need it."

"Keep it. I would take it back after you get your salary. Is it possible to walk the streets in rains with this slipper on?"

"Dada, I am fed up. How can I get a job at this age? I would have been relieved to leave this job. What godforsaken luck I have! Moreover, God did not give me a male child. You have to prepare for the daughter's marriage from the day she crosses fifteen. What do I earn that I would save? I do not do a job of fraudulent account-keeping that I would give her lot of jewelries from Senco Gold."

Samaresh uttered the last words a tad loudly as he was keeping the money in the pocket of his shirt. The distance between Ratan's and Baksi*da*'s table would be hardly ten yards.

2

A man dressed in a King's attire was sitting across the entrance of the shoe shop with an outstretched leg that had a new shoe on it. Underneath it was written, "Be a King as soon as you wear it". Samaresh has seen the advertisement in TV a couple of times. The moment he entered a young man of twenty-five approached him.

"Please come, Sir. How may I help you?"

The man was wearing a t-shirt of the shoe company. The way he came made sure that he had no work for a long time. Some ten customers were moving around in the entire shop. However, most of them were women. They had come just after dropping their children at school, or after fetching them from schools. From their demeanor you could tell that not all will buy shoes.

"Bhai, could you show me something of the wash-and-wear range?"

"You mean, Sandak? Wait, I would show you one."

The man went to the furthest end of the shop, craned his neck inside a cave-like door, spoke a few words with someone inside and came back with two packets.

"Under normal circumstances you would not get Sandaks now. I mean, those are not displayedat this time of the year, but now those would be. It has begun to rain a little from today. But, this is not a sandak, Sir. It's made of polymer but looks like original leather."

"What's the price?"

Samaresh asked the sales man as he examined the sandals. The man checked the packet and said,

"Rupees two-hundred, Sir."

"Bhai, isn't there any discount on offer?"

"No, Sir, we are a fixed-price shop. But, this slipper is best suited for office staffs like you. Just try it once. It's very comfortable. And it has been designed in a way so as not to disturb your natural footsteps. You would be able to hold on to your normal gait even on an uneven thoroughfare. Earlier, such sandals used to cost rupees six-thousand. Now we have brought the price down, within the reach of the middleclass. Sir, just take a walk. You will find that your whole personality has changed. You know, Sir, that shoes exalt a man's personality."

Samaresh slipped into the slippers and got ready for the trial. The touch of the sandal was soft. The man spoke unceasingly as he trailed him.

"Now look, Sir, can you find any similarity between the walking styles and personalities of AmitavBaachchan as he appears in his white shoes in *Don* and that of him when he enters with Kholapuri slippers on in *Dewar*? How attractive he was looking in *Don*! Look Sir, how handsome you are looking in this sandals."

"No bhai, show me something within rupees one-fifty. The price of rupees two-hundred is a bit on the higher side."

"Sir, listenonce to this younger brother of yours and buy the pair. You could get cheated only once, but I assure you that you would come to me after a week to talk of your splendid experience. On the streets, in the trains and buses, at your office people will think at least once before telling you something. I think, Sir, shoes make the personality of a man flourish. Just think, Sir, our Chief Ministermoves around in a white Hawaii slipper always. But what an influencing personality she has got! If she goes for any fancy shoes from tomorrow, her whole personality would take a beating."

Samaresh listened to the man, mesmerized. Must be a new entrant in this profession. Wants to prove his mettle in sales.

"Sir, then let me pack you this pair."

Samaresh could only nod.

"Bijoy*da*, one bill will have to be prepared. S 314…"

Samaresh put his hand on one of the shoulders of the man,

"Bhai, you will prosper in this profession."

3

The whole afternoon was spent in a good-for-nothing business. Some troubles related to construction syndicate … had one reached a settlement after taking the boss into confidence the problem would have been solved by now. No. You spend the whole day at the site and in the office of the syndicate without any food or drinks. Samaresh was in a vile mood today. He has pulled up the young lad of the Shaw's.

"Never enter into a fight with local boys."

"Even if they detain the truck carrying sand!"

"Did they detain your father's truck? It's company's vehicle. First inform the company. No need to visit in person. If they fracture your head the company will not do anything other than getting you admitted in a hospital. Do you understand my point? You are new. That's why I am telling all these for your benefit. Just see, the company will make them step back by tomorrow. Let rupees five lakh or so go down the drains; who is bothered? The customer will pay for the sum. How is the company affected?"

The lad stood speechless.

"Listen, you need not stay here until late at night today. Move out of this place with me."

The lad, without uttering a word, picked up his cloth-tiffin-bag and started to follow Samaresh. Samarsh felt a bit satisfied today. This lad has got really scared. Otherwise he is not the type to follow Samaresh without any protest. The boy argues a lot. Especially he has no respect for Samaresh. Today he must have got scared because of the syndicate bosses. But, the lad had faced them earlier. They created trouble to put their laborers on the roll during the laying of the foundation stone. The lad then had just joined. He tackled the police alone. Then? Suddenly Samaresh remembered the man at the shoe shop. "Your personality would undergo a metamorphosis." Has that really happened? Samaresh became a bit conscious. Yes, he could feel the difference, though a bit. He felt that he was bolder and stronger than before. He felt the same way when he came out of the theatre after watching an action flick of Hollywood when he was young.

"Ratanda, look how my new pair of sandals are."

The first thing that Samaresh did after entering the office was to place the sandals in front of Ratan's table.

Ratan pushed his chair back a bit and looked at the sandals.

"Oh! It's good."

He showed no further interest. Ratan pulled his chair back in place and went back to his work.

"What? Has anything happened in office?"

"No, nothing much."

"Tell me, what has happened?"

Samaresh after entering office did not watch the place. Now he took a look and found that the prevailing mood was somber. "Oh God! What has happened again?"

"Leave it. You had roamed the whole day. Take some rest and eat something."

"I ate some time ago. But, tell me please, what happened wrong?"
"You told me in the morning that you would not be able to work here for long. The list will perhaps begin with me."

Samaresh had never seen Ratan speak like this. Something big must have happened.

"Tell me, Ratan*da*, what has happened?"

"See, last month a payment had been made for a truckload of stone chips for the Baruipur project. Today we received the information that the material had never been delivered."

"Okay, but what has that to do with you?"

"Boss had called me and Baksi*da*. Baksi*da* told that I had made the payment without inquiring into the matter. But, you knowthat I release the payment only after Baksi*da*approves."

"How is our boss reacting now?

"What would he say? He needs the material by tomorrow or else…"

"Else?"

Ratan could not answer the question. He just let a sigh out.

"Sir, I am entering your cabin."

Samaresh did not wait for the boss' reply.

"Oh you! What did finally happen at Kasba?"

"I have spoken to them. They want to supply something. I have told them that bricks and sand were out of question now. We have already made our payments for those. Had they requested us before…"

"What did they say?"

"I have asked for a day's time from them and told them that our boss would inform them all that have to be said."

"But, why me? You only were tackling the situation."

"Sir, I am not the proprietor of the firm that I would take a call by myself."

Strange! What has happened to Samaresh? The words he spoke even surprised him. And the boss was acceptingall that he said.

"No, I am not going into that. You could have said something. Tell me what order we could give them?"

Samaresh was feeling uneasy. What is happening? How could the boss change absolutely in a span of six-seven hours? Once Samaresh thought of asking him. The next moment the words started ringingin his ears, "Sir, your personality will undergo a metamorphosis. On the streets, in the buses and trains, in the office people before telling you anything will…"

"The sanitary work has not been done yet, you could place some orders related to the sanitary items of the flat."

"All right. Give them a requisition slip tomorrow. And give them a check of rupees ten-thousand. Ask our people to check the materials before receiving the delivery."

"Okay,Sir."

Samaresh turned his back to leave the chamber but turned again to face the boss.

"Sir, may I tell you something?"

"Yes, go ahead."

"I know both Ratan*da* and Baksi*da* much more than you do. Did you ever think that how could one, in spite of getting almost the similar salary as the other, feed some four-hundred people in his daughter's wedding and present his daughter all hallmarked jewelries, while the other fails even to get his son admitted in a good school because of financial reasons? Would you like to believe that Ratan*da* has pocketed the commission after clearing the stone chip bill?"

Mr. Chowdhury lowered his head after attentively listening to Samaresh. He pushed his glass full of water towards Samaresh and said,

"Drink some water first. I know everything. Tomorrow I will take whatever action is required against Baksi*babu*. Actually he belongs to my father's era; I would not be able to do anything without talking to my father. Be sure, nothing will happen to Ratan."

"Sir, another issue. As per your order I will have to show the tickets of the bus to get the TA bills reimbursed, what if I travel in an auto rickshaw?"

"In that case you bring the bill to me and I will sign."

Samaresh took a long breath after coming out of the chamber. As if he had won a war. He then went back and leaned in his chair; he raised his right leg on his left and started to observe the new pair of slipper. The slipper was indeed charismatic. This slipper has done what he could not even dream of doing. What godly power could a brown colored number-seven pair of sandals have? He fished out the writing pad from his bag and began to prepare the TA bill. He would pin the tickets, and then submit the bill and take Ratan for a cup of tea downstairs. But the tickets? Where could the tickets go from the pocket of his shirt?

"Dada, book your ticket."

Samaresh was dozing off. In one blow everything seems to fall in place. He was tired after a hard day's work outside.

"How much is the ticket to Dharamatala?"

"From where?"

"Kasba."

"Eight rupees."

"And Chandni?"

"Ten."

"Then book up to Dharamatala."

He gave the conductor a ten-rupee note. The guy gave him a ticket and a rupees two coin in return. Until now the bus was not much crowded. The crowd swelled from RabindraSadan. All the passengers were Sealdah bound. Most were youngsters. May be they worked in the sales. Samaresh watched their legs. They had shining boots on. Over that the dark colored trousers and light colored shirts had changed the personalities of the young men. There was another boy standing in the front portion of the bus. The structure of his face wasn't bad. His entire face was covered in a beard and moustache. He had almost six month's uncut and unkempt hair on his head. He was wearing a low-cost, mud-soaked slipper made of plastic. He had a bag hanging from his shoulders. He must be a poet or something similar. The boy was a bit hesitant to stand among the rest of the boys. I think, it's nothing other than the fact the poet-like lad was suffering from an identity crisis in front of the other well clad boys. Samaresh felt satisfied. "It was perhaps a right decision to have bought those sandals."

"Ratan*da*, please take a look."

Samaresh spread his right leg towards Ratan.

Ratan took a glance once.

"It's good. Do not stand here for long. Go and meet Choudhuri*saheb*, he had looked for you twice. Why did you keep your phone switched off? We will talk more after office hours."

Samaresh once took a look around the office.

"Ratan*da*, the weather seems to be hot even now?"

"Yes!"

Samsaresh lowered his bag on the table and took a few gulps of water from the bottle. The moment he looked at the table next to him Ashim*da* made some gestures. Samaresh failed to understand. "What?" Ashim*da* raised his finger to the mouth in a bid to ask him to stay silent and pointed at Mr. Choudhury's chamber. The moment Samaresh tried to make a move towards him Baksi raised his head and said,

"After you have finished drinking water please go to the boss' chamber once and give me a portion of your salary every m"onth."

"Why Baksi*da*? What has happened?

"You would come to know that the moment you step into the cabin. All nuisances. I have been suffering from severe neck pain the whole day and every five minutes the boss queried, "Hasn't Samaresh come back?""

Mr. Choudhury was speaking to someone over the telephone. Seeing Samaresh he kept the receiver down and asked, "When did you come?"

"Just now, Sir."

"The site had been closed at 4 pm. Have you been roaming in the South City Mall? Or did you walk the entire distance?"

"No, Sir. I closed the site, sent the boy home and then returned. Had there not been traffic jam on the road I would have…"

"Your phone was switched off…"

"Yes, Sir, it has run out of charge."

"I called up the boy. He told me that he wound up the work and had left by 4 pm. And you were at that time…"

"What are you saying, Sir? I was at the syndicate's office around 4 pm."

"Samaresh*babu*, I thought my father had recruited all gentlemen in this office but I was not aware that he had reared a liar like you here. Listen, the Syndicate secretary did call me up half-an-hour ago. He told me that you have said you would let him know by six in the evening."

The boy had given him up! Samaresh's hands and legs were trembling in anxiety. This has been his problem since his childhood days. Even during minor altercations at school his entire body shook vigorously. For this he had never watched any East Bengal-Mohun Bagan match; he could neither watch the final of the last World Cup.

"And who asked you to say that instead of placing an order with them to supply sand and tiles we would ask them to supply sanitary materials?"

"Had I not said they would not have allowed the work to resume?"

"That would have been the concern of the company, me and the local police there. Did the company give you the responsibility to consider its all the good and evil. What would I do with you, can you tell me? You are not capable to do any in-house work and you complicate the outdoors responsibility given to you. Company almost pays you for doing nothing. This cannot go on for long."

The color of the sky visible beyond the office buildings in this area is red. It will rain in the night, perhaps. The tables in the office were slowly being vacated. Samaresh went and sat at his desk. Ashim*da* gently pressed him at the back before he left. Samaresh lifted his eyes from the table to see. As they left the office in groups they spoke to each other in a suppressed voice; some even laughed. Bishu, the resident of Rathtalla, looked at him to poke fun. Now he should not look up at that direction. Samaresh lowered his face. He wanted to lower it further from the table towards the floor. A pair of feet on the floor. There was a number-seven, brown colored sandak underneath the feet. It was still written on it, "Become a king the moment you wear it."

The Assassinator

I have never been to this area before. Even in the middle of this half-darkness, the exterior lighting of this house seems to be interesting, but as you enter you get a feel of a foreign restaurant and not of an office. Some of us were sitting on a light sponge-fitted bench, and as we sat in the semi darkness for sometime our eyes got accustomed to it. Now I could make out the faces around. We were there in a way as if we all knew each other, but as the moment was not a joyous one we failed to recognize each other. There was an elderly man unaffected by everything around. It seemed there might be something that was bugging him more than anything else. The man was showing signs of irritation. In itself, to stay calm appeared to be a problem to him. He came as close to me as possible and asked in a hushed tone,

"Sir, do you know?"

I lifted my eyes to look at him.

"A murderer is roaming in this area. He looks like a gentleman, but he kills in a very ungentle way. I have been so afraid! Even I thought a couple of times whether to come here or not!"

I couldn't get what he meant, but the man did not notice. He continued on his own…

"The bastard rips the veins with glass, it seems! Aren't you noticing how quiet everybody here is out of fear?"

I carefully ran my eyes all around. I could not measure the expression of the faces around, but what if it is true! I had butterflies in my underbelly the moment I thought that. I was curious and inquired:

"How many have gone by now?"

"Twelve!"

The lady seated beside me unobtrusively threw in the word.

"No, no! Not that many. Six persons have gone. Of these two had been killed in such a way that no one could identify them."

The man rectified the faulty information like a competent news reporter.

"I told you about the number of people who had gone inside."

It appeared that the lady was a bit disgusted.

"Oh! Tell me that."

I felt desperate for a smoke. I have heard in these big offices smoking is strictly prohibited. The wooden door was kept closed from inside. Those who had entered were not coming out. It seemed there was another way for their exit. As a result not even one secret was coming out. These were really clever people! And for the first time the door parted. A boy, wearing a knee-length pant came out. I would not be able to describe him, for his face was not clearly visible. The moment he came out he questioned,

"Has Biplab come? Has anyone seen him?"

The very gentleman seated next to me replied like an idiot,

"No! Nothing of that sort has come as yet! Why? Are we expecting it to appear?"

They boy did not respond to the man; he only raised his finger and beckoned me in.

Inside, there was a blue light pervading across the entire room. The light overflowed from the table and in a series of small waves was reaching everywhere in the room. I was not aware of the name of the man who was seated just opposite to me. Neither did I have any intention to know. People look like outlines in light, I have noticed. He was constantly asking questions. The attitude was such that he had no interest in listening to the answers, but he was listening to every reply attentively. The questions were ordinary. Almost like some biography. After answering one question I was promptly forgetting the previous one. In the meanwhile my mind was egging me on to do some mischief.

"What is your favorite work?"

"To change the lines in a poem."

"Like?"

"*Let there be rain here round the year / Let the clouds graze here like cows…*"

"You are a dangerous man, it seems! I think you are not apt for this job."

"I agree, but I badly need the job."

"There are certain rules for our job, I mean, certain conditions…"

"Like?"

"For example we will make the rules here and if needed we will ourselves break the rules. No interference of the people outside will be entertained."

"There is no one to shout for me, because I also do not do it for anyone."

"Next rule, you cannot do politics here, and we control the politics of one's personal life, rather!"

"This is a bit taxing. One worker each trailing so many workers and another following them … no, I can think no more. You carry on."

"There's nothing much to think of. We are here to think, you got it? Rule number three. You have to sit for a test to exit the organization as you have to undergo a test to enter it, this unless we are sure that you are no longer controlled by your brain. And if you try to break any of these rules, we will take action. I have a special responsibility – you may say, I'm especially trained for this duty. Have you heard that some people from this area have gone missing for a few days now?"

"Yes, but the word is not perhaps "missing," but "murder.""

"No, it's missing. Does anyone know the destination of men after their death?"

"No."

"Right! After death everyone goes missing. And the people who have gone missing have been our workers."

I screamed in ecstasy. That serial killer was sitting in front of me! I could ask for his autograph, if I wanted to get it. And I can startle the talkative man sitting outside by showing him that. I was, in fact, shouting out of joy. Perhaps this was not right. It was not proper to sit in an office and break its rules! I might be punished for this. What could be the outcome? I had butterflies in my underbelly. The specially trained man to handle such things, who was seated in front suddenly broke a glass into pieces. His intention was not proper, I guessed. I would rather come later to ask for his autograph! It seemed idiotic to stay sitting there for nothing. The lady, who sat by my side outside also said, "Run away!" But I failed to understand what kind of escape would fit the scene. Would I say a great dialogue that might appear partly to be a riddle and a joke? Could I unnerve the man by kissing him? However, finally, I pushed the chair back and rose. I considered this suitable for this scene. If needed I would probably ask some director later on to find if this was right or wrong!

When I came out in the verandah outside I could not decide which side to go. I felt like going for a toss. I was confused and decided to run to the left. Here 'run' meant the fast-paced walk that I was accustomed to. But I got exhausted pretty soon. There were rows of rooms that had their doors shut. There was no time to check the number of the rooms. I realized that it was important to stay alive. I had, until now, seen nothing in life. At least I would see these rooms for once.

The rooms appeared to be a bit darker from the outside. Or was it not! Those were completely dark.

In reality my eyes were out of the tune. This was the reason I failed to notice the difference between darkness and not-that-darkness. I failed to realize what all were there inside the room. I felt that something moved away very close to my back. As if I heard the sound of his moving body! Did it arrive before I managed? How did it enter into the room? Was there a door in each room? But, how would it know about my arrival? My mind was gradually getting tired. I felt thirsty, and the tremors of a body within my body. Like something that a man feels before waking up from a dream.

It's dead into the night now. But my sleep has broken. The doors and windows became a bit alert seeing me waking up at an odd hour. They are looking at me without fluttering their eyelashes. But they were afraid of asking me any question. In the morning I had broken one side of the window following a fight with my mother.

As if the unemployed had no value! "Why do you sleep so much?"

"Oh God! What will I do if there aren't any job? Even the unemployed have to pass their time. We cannot even go for a cinema."

"Tomorrow is the last day to draw the ration. There isn't any money. The ration card might expire now."

"Let it lapse. Let them round up all the non-citizens. For how long one can live after being chased?"

I stepped on the floor after leaving the bed. The floor was as cold as ice.

"Have you got the job?"

Someone asked the question. It was perhaps the south-facing window.

"No."

"Oh! Your dad has exhausted his inhaler. He is suffering from breathlessness since evening."

At the corner of the room my mother always keeps a stick to ward off the cats. I will sleep with the stick by my bedside tonight. If the murderer comes after I fall asleep, I will certainly injure his limbs this time.

Note: "Biplab" is a common male-name and it is a Bengali word that means revolution. The lines of the poem mentioned here, have been derived from the famous poem "Abani Bari Acho" by the legendary Bengali poet Shakti Chattopadhyay.

About the author

Born in the year 1984, Bitan Chakraborty studied Software Development from Jadavpur University, Calcutta, and later he spent eight years learning and actively participating in Theater under the auspices of the esteemed Jangam. Bitan does not quite like to be marked as an Engineer, and he dreams to live a life of a theater artiste. He is the founder of Hawakaal Publishers. He has authored two books in the Bengali language: *Obhinetar Journal (Journal of an Actor)*, and *Santiram-er Cha (Tea by Santiram)*, which has received much critical acclaim in India. *Bougainvillea and Other Stories* has been derived from the constituent stories of *Santiram-er Cha.*

About the translator

Pranab Ghosh is a journalist, blogger and writer. He writes both in English and Bengali. He specializes in short stories, but also writes poetry. He has worked in media organizations like HT and Eenadu India. Ghosh has co-authored *Air & Age*, a collection of poetry, along with Tanmoy Bhattacharjee. He is a guest faculty of Rabindra Bharati University and teaches Journalism. He lives in Calcutta with his wife, daughter and mother.

www.ingramcontent.com/pod-product-compliance
Lightning Source LLC
Chambersburg PA
CBHW051454130726

47987CB00005B/2301